D0887007

POLITICAL MORALITY

POLITICAL MORALITY
A GENERAL THEORY OF POLITICS

by

PHILIP S. HARING

SCHENKMAN PUBLISHING COMPANY, INC.
Cambridge, Massachusetts

Library of Congress Catalog Card Number 71-118575

Copyright © 1970

BY SCHENKMAN PUBLISHING CO. INC.
Cambridge, Massachusetts 02138

For

Jacqueline and Tori Haring

Acknowledgements

Debate at faculty seminars and with colleagues from all departments of Knox College, as well as student enthusiasm for continual discussion, have made Knox an ideal environment for working out a general theory. It seems too little merely to be grateful for all that members of this community have given me; learning among them is a privilege beyond acknowledgement.

Numerous people have been of great help to me in writing and publishing this book. My wife's encouragement made possible my putting these thoughts on paper and together we edited the final manuscript. Eloise Wilkinson kindly did the typing. J. David Singer, Christian Bay, and Roman Hedges read the entire book and offered helpful criticism in addition to much appreciated support. Alfred Schenkman has demonstrated his talent for swift and efficient publication. His editor, Cynthia McClintock, most conscientiously reviewed every sentence before the manuscript went to galley. I want also to acknowledge my teachers, who had time for my questions, and those rare, great writers whose works forever inform us.

P. S. H.

CONTENTS

PREFACE

There are two reasons why this book should be of interest at this time. The first is that quite unexpectedly the leading behavioralist writers have begun asking for speculative general theory. It was hoped over the last half century that when enough empirical research could be done, a pattern of findings would inductively suggest some entirely new perspective upon political events. That new perspective, grounded upon undeniable evidence, would then in itself become a commonly accepted general theory of politics and perhaps of social behavior as a whole. But instead, and despite vast efforts at methodological sophistication, our empirical findings have been mere footnotes to hypotheses put forth two or more centuries ago. No new perspective concerning substantive politics has emerged. Yet there is need for new perspectives simply because the terms within which seventeenth and eighteenth century political theory was written (natural law, the State of Nature, inherent political rights) no longer fit current presuppositions. Either the essential claims of former theory must be reworked and made relevant, or else by some imaginative leap we must transcend the walls of our heritage and grasp new hypotheses that, at first, we may recognize only intuitively and then, with reexamination of empirical findings, be able to apply such new hypotheses in practical political existence. This book purports to be such a contribution. While I was writing it there seemed no hope that anyone would ever again include speculative philosophy among respectable endeavors of social scientists. But at this moment there is no question that the door is again open.

The second reason why this book should be of interest is an equally sudden concern for social morality. The roots of our former unconcern reach back to the failure of the Reformation, to the impossibility at that time of reconciling competing social ethics, and to the conviction that every man is his own private theologian so that a bland toleration of any and all behavior alone seemed to protect individual conscience. Self-interest replaced social interest unless the two happily coincided. The interest of princes was separate from that of individuals, for which reason individuals were urged to resist governments. Yet experience has reaffirmed an older wisdom that unless princes act to protect individuals, individuals will likely destroy one another; and likewise, that unless princes are bounded by some moral discipline superior to their own ambitions, they will destroy each other and each other's citizenry. Seventeenth and eighteenth century political theories emerging from the shambles of the Reformation have been of no use here. Political practice has increasingly ignored those theories; the modern social welfare state grew in response merely to the availability of new and seemingly unlimited means for material welfare without any moral or ethical rationalization beyond meeting reputedly popular demands for more equal incomes and formal social status. Some entirely new, tough minded, insightful perspective is required that depends neither upon private morality publicly irrelevant nor upon public amorality blind to private welfare. Again, this book purports to answer that need.

In attempting to supply a political theory and to answer how morality is relevant to governmental activity, I have been very general and inclusive rather than detailed and specific. This is not a difficulty with, but rather the whole point and purpose of, general theory. General theory is not a blueprint for immediate policy decisions, nor even an explanation of world conditions at particular times. It should not be confused with historical analysis of trends and developments. If so, Locke would have traced the growth of British constitutional evolution from William the Conqueror to his own day; instead he postulated a single dichotomy between a pre-societal State of Nature and fully developed polities as if he had no idea of history, and all this despite the temptation to set Filmer's history right. Locke's ahistorical, "unrealistic," contemporarily irrelevant model has served as a guide to constitution-building for several centuries while innumerable empirical studies of partisan political programs and of institutional development and procedures have all faded from view to become curiosities of intellectual history. The generalizations of general theory must be loose enough to admit the widest variations of future political fact while sufficiently provocative to suggest particular institutional changes and political programs that the theory itself refrains from specifying in detail. Montesquieu's historical citations are ignored while his widest generalizations have proved fruitful. Machiavelli's appeal for a unified Italy is a curiosity while his most outrageous passages on political psychology continue to intrigue and challenge our imaginations. Marx's economic history was a mere springboard for his theory of a new sort of revolution.

There are grave methodological problems imbedded in the above but I leave these to others since for a half century we have done little else than publish manifestoes concerning how we will discover the full substance of politics if only we can decide how to do it. I want merely to explain what general theory is about and why I am unconcerned with grounding my theory upon historical data or with applying it specifically to current problems. I deviate from this rule in the last two chapters simply because the immediate problem of suicidal war is so terrible that a few practical suggestions are in order. Likewise the ahistorical, analytic, generalizing nature of general theory separates this endeavor from the more usual scholarly concern with justifying every statement by reference to research findings, to others' similar or opposed opinions, and with pursuing intellectual controversy. A general theory is properly interesting in itself aside from any authority for it which might be gained by tracing its connections with or dissociation from other theories and theorists. It is true that lack of footnotes obscures the sources of my thought, yet since my debt to others does not lie in borrowing from them but in their teaching me to be my own man, I cannot pretend to have derived my model from theirs. The effort has been to avoid distraction by contemporary events and insofar as possible to stretch the limits of my culture-boundedness. Yet I wanted to speak for concrete human beings caught up in homely and recognizable situations. Even so, this book is not at all a statement of personal preferences for a world that I want to inhabit. Quite unintentionally and contrary to what I privately value, the logic of believable moral limitations upon political action led to setting aside nearly everything held dear in the Anglo-American constitutional tradition. That unconscious strategy was necessary if my theory would on one hand have any universality, and on the other hand support, and foreshadow the difficulties inherent in, any post-Anglo-American world polity. The result is a series of assumptions about political mankind and political events wholly independent of previous political speculation. It therefore becomes obvious why contemporary empirical research has been of slight help because it is based upon implicit assumptions with little relationship to mine.

The book constitutes a return to very ancient inquiries that are still essential to understanding what politics is about and what can be expected from it, where we are in the world and what we can do about our situation. But this is no theory of natural laws; nor does it rely upon conscience or any wave of future social-economic-political development. It presents a new perspective on politics and government derived from a reconsideration of how politics originates, the relationship of rulers and ruled, the psychological make-up of political leaders, and a new concept of justice. It acknowledges how modern states are managed and suggests how international peace could be established.

P. S. H.

Knox College   1970

"True politics I look on as a part of moral philosophy, which is nothing but the art of conducting men right in society and supporting a community among its neighbors."

John Locke to Lady Mordaunt

"For though in all places of the world men should lay the foundation of their houses on the sand, it could not thence be inferred that so it ought to be."

Thomas Hobbes, *Leviathan*, Bk. II, Ch. 20

" . . . under the present circumstances of human society both the structure and form of governments as well as the power which public authority wields in all the nations of the world, must be considered inadequate to promote the universal common good."

Pope John XXIII, *Pacem in Terris*, Sect. 135

I.

THE GENERAL PROBLEM
OF HUMAN EXISTENCE

Humanity forever hesitates on the brink of its next step forward. There are more than enough ideas of how to accomplish our objectives. Yet we hesitate to trust ourselves and each other to move ahead and reach those objectives. We distrust our capacities to make our lives over, to improve our lot. Part of this hesitancy must have arisen in childhood when repeatedly our parents proved us wrong as now we prove our children wrong. Those scars from our vulnerability to error were bandaged over with pride and truculence that in turn we offset with renewed caution. At school and later, having once distrusted ourselves, we cling to whatever formulas for living and behaving that teachers pump-prime into us. Mankind has always been the victim of its own ideas about itself as put forth in each generation in each town and city on the earth's surface, in every culture by teachers of that culture, its perpetuators. Teachers are a hapless lot. They hand along what they were taught plus some reflections of the day's mood which hopefully will be useful for getting forward in the world. Nearly everything that they say is found in a textbook. Nor could it be otherwise if a whole society of persons is to be offered some common basis for behavior toward one another. Absence of such enculturation would make cooperation impossible and prevent the maintenance of any societies anywhere.

The contents of a textbook are not wholly the author's fault. He must satisfy parents, school officials, even the government which licenses and often subsidizes education, and anyway has an interest in the new generation's view of the society which that government is administering—the author must satisfy everyone that he is not corrupting youth. It is a very serious matter. It is not a question of truth or of science, the science of how to train minds most efficiently or the science of how to conduct social affairs most effectively. It is a matter of moral choice: of what youth ought to hear, of what is good for them, of how well they may fare in the world after imbibing this or that doctrine of social behavior. The textbook writer has to play it safe. He cannot condemn too critically the ways and thoughts of his students' elders lest students disdain their heritage, or read too closely and precisely what past philosophers actually taught lest the pitiful shallowness of contemporary interpretations equally engender students' disdain. These instructions would corrupt youth. No human society can withstand such corruption—because disdainful superciliousness erects no alternative foundation of hope on which to risk further behavior. Unless elders endorse new hopes and thus establish a new orthodoxy, old hopes however hollow cannot reasonably be discarded. The old might yet succeed. Less hesitancy and more trust might rescue the day. Civilization is no more than belief that we have transcended a brutish existence. Undermining that belief, or failing to sustain it, corrupts not only the means by which human affairs are improved but by which they survive.

People are deficient instruments for furthering their own welfare. Though their goals have failed them a thousand times, people need to reaffirm these guides or perish. This necessary disingenuousness inhibits youth as much as it formerly did their parents, who now are merely accustomed to it. For this reason, social goals are less questioned than insistently propounded. They are, for us, the attainment of peace, prosperity, health, and the end of exploitation. We have not trained our children to live in a world already peaceful or prosperous, healthy or non-exploitative. We dare not because we do not understand what peaceableness entails, and fear what would happen to them cast out defenseless in the bellicose world of their elders. Better that they hope for a peace not yet attained than be corrupted into supposing that we would tolerate its actual occurrence. And yet we would not disillusion them toward ourselves since we need their trust in us to support our self-confidence. In these ways the blind lead the blind in every time and place.

I have noted this phenomenon at some length because it lies at the center of human deficiency, explains why we fail to remake our behavior all in a day. We are bound not by a dispensable past but by the indispensable present of justifiable hesitation. I also note this phenomenon's universality to demonstrate that there are universal human experiences. Yet this and other universals are differently presented by every generation of scholars, each using its own language of concepts to sustain and explore parallel insights. The alteration of images from one language of concepts to another suggests that there is an endless flux of irreconcilable cultures independent of one another, though successive and foreshadowed in their predecessors. Awareness of this difficulty persuades many people that it is hopeless to seek certainty about anything trans-cultural. Yet differing conceptual languages merely disguise rather than refute what has been clearly universal, such as hesitancy to act and to trust ourselves, and our fear of corrupting youth. I seek those universals in this book. If they exist, they are the stuff from which any reliable philosophy would be deduced. And if they do not, my various theses are not destroyed; each can stand alone.

I assume that implicit in all these universals is a concern for personal and social survival. This is necessarily a constant concern. In primitive economies it derived from the fear that if the next generation should fail to maintain those economies, the old would starve, unable to labor. In our own time the fear is of societal changes making the world of our old age impossible for us to accept, so unfamiliar as to unnerve us. Moreover, the means of our survival need to be rationalized or we lose all élan to go forward in our daily tasks; why should we struggle? Rationalizations of capacity to surmount particular and purely contemporary threats to survival must embrace more than just those threats or else new ones will find us disarmed and vulnerable. Rationalizations must have the character of universal solutions to our dilemmas. For this reason a social theory is hardly persuasive which does not at least attempt to stand on universal grounds.

Among these rationalizations or beliefs I cite two that appear to me untrustworthy although they were carried around the globe by eighteenth and nineteenth century propagators of our culture and have become common sense if not self-evident truths for humanity as a whole. The first belief is an assumption that when any human good, material or otherwise, is scarce it will acquire value in human eyes, and that anything of value will be sought, will have market value. The result is supposed to be that somehow, somewhere a few or many people will be inspired to supply more of this rarity, make it more commonly available, thus bringing down its price in whatever coinage it is traded, and finally in this way fulfill human desires. An idea invented by early economists to explain the supposed fact of gradual material betterment in their time, it is a magnificent formula. If there is not enough of something, such as peace or prosperity, it is assumed in this model that no one yet has had time to supply it or has not yet found ways to supply it. But

4

all will be well in the end. Negligence will be overcome by
the pressures of demand. It is only a matter of political scientists discovering the way of peace, or of psychologists finding
the true dynamics of marital bliss, or of economists prescribing
for the ills of the poor. I may seem sarcastic and yet I believe
a bit of this myself, at least to some extent. And I write this
book partly to correct my own views of our folklore. Governments everywhere are expending billions through universities
and in aid-to-the-unfortunate upon this very assumption—that
scarcities of all good things exist, that governments should not
oppose the inevitable trend of this inevitable law of scarcity-
fulfillment, that by encouraging ever greater activity the most
glaring of contemporary scarcities are bound to be overcome.
The implication of this first belief is that mankind's difficulties have centered wholly upon scarcity. Where there is not
enough of something, people suffer the lack of it. When they
have enough of what they lack, they will be able to enjoy themselves. Anyone can understand this simple conclusion. It is
not that people stupidly refuse to recognize good fortune, or
that good fortune is an elusive concept; the formula for successful living plainly states that of course a starving man wants
food and will know when his stomach is full. Nor is there a
problem in fulfilling all human goods since, whenever a need
appears, someone will turn to filling it.

Though we all believe this formula to some extent, we all
know that it is nonsense. Any other answer, nevertheless, is
hard to imagine. We know that the securely rich, famous, or
otherwise replete have seldom if ever confessed themselves ful-
filled. Their former poverty often seems to them a time of
greater happiness than their present wealth .Certainly no vastly
learned man confesses satisfaction with his knowledge. Is it
merely that earlier scarcities are replaced by others at a later
time? To some extent this is true. And yet must there not

be some lacks whose fulfillment would complete existence for us, the rest being unimportant or peripheral? Or is the human condition such that we must be perpetually dissatisfied, all dreams of fulfillment an empty folly? The last answer has often been given, though without dampening our anticipations. Or is the trouble at the very center of this scarcity-fulfillment formula: that instead of there being someone, somewhere capable of meeting demands for a scarcity, very few and often no one is able to think past the mental blocks which originally created the scarcity? Most ills are accepted as unavoidable because no one has thought of a way around them. It is therefore untrue that absence or scarcity of a solution to some human ill inspires its discovery. Mankind's difficulties do not center upon scarcity but upon lack of imagination, initiative, and of willingness to reshape the culture toward mankind's vague desire for a better existence. Scarcity exists but it is primarily one of talents for living intelligently rather than any absence of time and resources for using talents already available. Were this not true statesmen would long ago have given us international peace and we would have welcomed it without hesitation.

The means to peace are obvious: to declare it, to disarm, to reap the benefits. Anyone supposing that whole peoples wish conflict and thus force statesmen to make war misreads all the evidence. How does any child come to know even the presence of other nations except through textbooks written as I have described? How does any citizen of one nation come to suppose another nation hostile except through press reports of what government leaders surmise? And how does a statesman surmise another's hostility? Through reports of his ambassadors and secret agents, and through conversation with his enemy. Perhaps it is true after all that peace waits upon the genius of these statesmen and their associates to discover and supply the ingredients of peaceful rule for which a market has long existed. It is a much more difficult question whether during peacetimes people have consumed or appreciated peace with sufficient satisfaction to convince statesmen that there is no market for war.

The scarcity-fulfillment model is breaking down. Contrary to the model we have to admit that markets are created; they have no spontaneous existence even in the case of food for the starving. A man may well starve for being told that he must diet. Markets for peace and war are both engineered. Scarcities of trust between people are created; for example, an incredulous public is told that its friends of yesterday are today's enemies or that it has demanded unanimously what it had not even thought of until this moment. But are there limits to our being victims of propaganda? No doubt, but as for our more sophisticated beliefs and rationalizations like that about scarcity, I know no limits to credulity. Our problems, then, are not simple, to be solved through a self-generating process of knowing our lacks and fulfilling them, but are far more difficult.

A second very local and historically parochial belief about human behavior is that humans require only to be freed from interference by one another, by constraints of any kind, to become truly themselves—which is assumed to be a blissful state of freedom in expressing and acting upon all their potentialities. However limited are those potentialities, they presumably would fully occupy and delight their possessor if only they could be exercised. A perfect world would be frictionless; a unique psyche within each person would bloom like a desert flower. It is upon this assumption that statesmen have conceived the need or market for expansion of influence or national boundaries; those remaining alive after a war of defense-against-constriction would presumably be able to move about and fulfill potentialities previously inhibited. The supposition that all other statesmen must necessarily follow the same reasoning leads

7

to preventive wars, or wars to prevent preventive wars. But shortcomings of the model are obvious. Were everyone free from others' interference, they would reveal not their inhibited potentialities but their own immense deficiencies of talent for conceiving or doing very much of anything. Better that people deceive themselves about their creative capacities than that they be humiliated by the vacuous stretches of their pitiful inadequacies. We are not self-sufficient. Everything that I have said about our need for rationalization, for reassurance, and about our deficiences of talent confirms our interdependence. Freedom from interference is the last burden that we should be asked to bear. What talents we have are no doubt developed in response to others' needs, although mere response to challenge is not enough or else peace and prosperity would long ago have superseded war and poverty.

Rather, it is because of our interdependence and our aid of one another, through application of our very unequal and varied talents, that awareness and expressions of our unique selves arise, and that we grow into human beings able to survive together. This point cannot be over-stressed. At least it is the rock on which this book is erected. Models of automatic scarcity-fulfillment, or of an inherent requirement to live independently of one another, alike suppose a population of rational, self-sufficient, self-disciplined persons whom I have never met. Human existence remains for me a problem of finding means to the end of beneficial interdependence.

That is the problem. But solutions of human existence concern only individuals, not humanity at large. Solutions are for each individual to seek throughout his life and attain at this or that turning of it; there is no general solution of the whole human dilemma for everyone collectively. A state of war may provide one man with opportunities that solve pressing problems of his life; he may learn enough about how people die, about fear, bravery, and the capacity for bearing pain to enrich his understanding for the rest of his days. But that personal solution raises the problem of others' welfare, their good versus his, for which there is no over-all solution. Solutions to human problems are always personal, culture-bound, relative to particular situations. In contrast to these is the general problem of human existence to which all such particular solutions are subsidiary and upon which they depend. This collective social problem hangs without conclusion or resolution; it extends backward throughout history and forward to the end of the human race. This problem is essentially political. It is the integration and management of people's diverse talents in order to make possible (without guaranteeing) everyone's working out his own evolving situation, including even his awareness of it.

This perpetual problem of mankind's existence is the care of the human community. Care of community lies at the base of everything else ascribable to humans and is, therefore, primary over all other human phenomena. It could not be otherwise. Coming upon each other with our needs, unable to do without each other, we have to find some means of integrating, perhaps reconciling, certainly arranging and managing all our scattered lacks and capacities in order to achieve individual goals without damaging our ability to live together. Care of these relationships is the political function. Politics could not have been invented as a form of social behavior before there were human relationships needing integration and management. Human relationships as we know them require the purpose and definition which political action alone provides. Politics and political organization are thus inherent in the human enterprise; before there was politics there was no mankind as we understand mankind to be. It is plausible that the border between persons and other animals lies precisely at this point

9

where conscious integration and management of social relationships supersedes genetically determined associative behavior.

I seem to say that politics is independent of particular forms of social organization, that it is as necessary for a family as for a nation. I mean just that. Moreover I find no evidence or suggestion of differences of kind between the most simple and complex institutions. Leadership may pass from one to another member of a family and back again, and be more formalized in larger social organizations; but such differences do not alter the function served. There is thus no need to construct a typology of political organizations. The elements of politics appear to me to originate in the general human condition of mutual dependence (true also of other creatures, though for many possible reasons other creatures have not adopted political behavior comparable to ours). These elements did not arise from historical events such as the development of Roman law or of Anglo-American constitutionalism or, within a different perspective, from the genius of Plato or Confucius; political and intellectual history embodies only particular expressions of these elements. The human condition allows so little variation in the means of governing that differences between the constitutional structure of various regimes are largely deceptive; they hardly affect the capacity of those regimes to integrate or manage social relationships, or to achieve justice. I will therefore devote only minor attention to the delusion that one or another so-called "form of government" is superior.

Arising from a general human condition and independent of particular forms of social organization, is politics, as I conceive it, the integration and management of every human relationship or only of certain relationships? Our human condition is interdependence, and politics concerns only the care of that interdependence, of the community or potential community implied thereby. Politics is unconcerned with relationships irrelevant to some community. But since almost every community is interdependent with others, what we call "government" includes authority over sub-communities such as families, commercial enterprises, professions (as well as over its own self-regulation). "Government" is therefore superior in authority over all regulative activities; the integration and management of all economic and social endeavor must be governmentally initiated or at least sanctioned. For this reason whatever is essential for governing a community as a whole will be found true of governing any part of the community, although not everything done in order to govern all of a community's activities is needed to govern each of them. This being so, my interest in political morality does not require examining lesser instances of it than exist in an entire community or polity; nor did anyone living before the present age of discrete social science disciplines imagine otherwise. Only recently have we lost perspective upon the unity and simplicity of human affairs.

II.

SOCIAL SYSTEMS FOR FALLIBLE PERSONS

We are interdependent because our talents vary enormously; each of us needs what others might supply. I do not have to argue that no one set down on an uninhabited island survives through native wit but only through the skills he was taught prior to his landing on the island; nor could he be alive except for his parents; nor could his parents have led him to become a human being except for a culture which taught them how to do it; nor would that culture have existed except for the work of tens of thousands whose ideas of what could be done resulted in a human way of living. So here we are—humans by virtue of living in a pre-existing culture. My model postulates a culture. But I cannot believe that any culture is perceived as the same collection of ideas by any two persons in that culture, because culture is not a phenomenon outside our bodies or minds. Culture is various ideas carried in the mind, used by those who carry them, and therefore given an individual stamp. Thus culture is not singular except as a convenience of speech and conception. Culture as a totality never exists. There are only your ideas and mine and others' which we try to understand and compare, especially with regard to their overlap and congruence. That there is any similarity in our ideas is explained by the labor of our teachers who engender a similar picture of things in our minds, though with different meaning and significance to each of us. The same is true of a foreman who instructs a group under his direction; cooperation on the work-project is possible to the degree that the boss' words are similarly understood. Yet both the beauty and the difficulty of this situation are immediately apparent. No one will ever know precisely what anyone else means, even while each will understand enough of another's hopes, fears, and abilities that integration of diverse talents-for-conception-and-action results. And that result is our way of living or culture though no one experiences or looks back upon it as the same phenomenon. It is beautiful in its usefulness, inhibiting and terrifying when we realize that what we call a shared experience is different for each of us. We are alone together, yet together in knowing something of which we can speak as if it were the same day and hour for each. Lovers embroider upon this dilemma throughout the whole range of written records, and enemies destroying each other feel more akin with each other than with those waiting for them at home.

Due to this situation there is an inherent tendency for every society to suggest that everyone should share more or less equally in all experiences, so that everyone will see how events come about and develop a certain companionship; the society would not then rely for survival upon its more experienced members. This notion of equality of experience and contribution is never likely to die out because it is so obvious, such a good answer to the problems of community survival and individual dignity. Yet it is absurd on its face. The very young and the senile have to be excused from sharing equal burdens with the rest. An enormous and irreconcilable difference of depth and direction and emotional tone colors the apparently similar thoughts of men and women, and forever makes them unequal. Individual variations of sensory and motor skills, of capacity for abstract thought, of patience, of openness to conflicting testimony cause all those absolute inequalities among persons which we call personality and which determine the significance of each person. It would therefore be impossible to mold or force everyone to experience equally either a few or all events. People are not equal nor should they be treated so—as if the impatient were to be reshaped through some educational or punitive process and made equal in forbearance with others, or vice versa. The task is too great and the consequences for everyone would be ruinous, since the society would be deprived of what precisely allows it to be a viable community.

What makes a community viable is what people can do for each other, not what they can do for themselves. If everyone came into the world fully grown, mature, totally knowledgeable (whatever that means) then our experiences would be truly the same, since all of us would know everything knowable: what is happening at any moment and what else is not happening, and why. Our fate is not only to be at different stages of maturity with regard to the culture in which we live, but also that in no culture can we know very much lying behind and ahead and to either side of that culture: the most knowing man is still pathetically ignorant of what is or is not happening to him from other perspectives than that of his own culture, or even of his own personality. He is in a parlous situation; he needs everyone's help.

By way of illustration I propose a very simplified model where there is no scarcity of material goods. In this model people are not fed with manna from heaven. They must request fulfillment of their needs but those are fully and regularly met through organization of necessary work. In this situation might not everyone supply himself by his own labor? Many might but in my model few, if any, find that it makes sense to do so. Division of labor permits specialized skills from whose products everyone benefits. Almost nothing is consumed by him who produces it; nearly everyone's work is exchanged. The reason is very simple. Diversity of skills due to age, sex, and inclination and the shortcomings of individual interpretations of what each in his own corner of the culture has provided, makes it better that no one try to rely only on what little he can do for himself. This remains true even if everyone could learn everyone else's skills, a feat doubtful if not impossible. No one could ever then rest from trying to become universally proficient within the culture's bounds. There would be no leisure nor any learning from one another. Interdependence due to inequalities of every sort is thus a very happy circumstance, nothing to regret or seek to alter.

Yet this condition, which I take to be inherent, yields a social significance. It is that people hereby depend upon some system for obtaining what they cannot and should not supply for themselves. Dependence on a system or plan of social organization spells trouble right away. While it is beneficial for people to depend on one another since dependence gives occasion for companionship and interaction—all the good things of living —yet also to depend on some plan, some system of prearranged cooperative behavior, is inhibiting and frustrating. To be caught in a system is to be imprisoned by it, forced to benefit from interdependence whether or not one wishes it. Nor can we scrap whatever systems of behavior encircle us and begin afresh, for any system is necessarily an outgrowth of previous ones and those in turn of yet previous systems, and backward through time to the beginning of things; in order for any of us to be alive and human, some system of behavior or culture had to instruct our parents how to bring us into a human community. Being thus instructed, whatever we do or plan to do differently is always a modification of something that went before and which becomes our starting place. Spontaneity is thus limited; our notions of the necessary or the feasible are culture-bound. Yet so what? Old patterns of behavior should fit us easily, having been brought up within their bounds. But that has never been so. No system of behavior will ever match any single person's mood at any moment, leading him to desire this or that, to act or not act; therefore no system fits anyone's desires except as he determines that he must or will fit himself to that system's demands.

The peculiar result is that a community cannot expect to find among its members a common denominator of everyone's wishes, unless it were a statistical finding foreign to anyone's actual wants. If everyone possessed essentially the same needs and desires, consulting together would soon reveal this commonness among them. They could then establish laws or agreements about what they would seek and (putting aside how they might seek it) joyfully proceed. But, because none of us has the same perceptions, experience, or talents, such an event is impossible. Or, to put it another way, since people are so differently endowed, no dictator could invent a system of behavior satisfying even a substantial minority. It was therefore only by assuming that everyone has the same, or similar, or at least reconcilable interests, and then by brain-washing them into believing it, that a "common will" was ever plausible. Such brain-washing takes place and does result in politicization, as I call it, but for quite other reasons than any pre-existing common interests, talents, or will. What the discoverer of the "general will," Rousseau, actually meant was that if people did not possess similar intentions of a most general kind, no society could exist. Rousseau's doctrine was believed by men anxious to find some happy resolution of their manifest differences of view and capacity. Over the last two centuries people have tried to pattern their perceptions to that doctrine, to the supposed commonness of their loves, hates, desires. But to no avail.

Instead, over those centuries varieties of opinion have multiplied; the intensity of emotions may not have deepened but their subtlety and sophistication certainly have, proportionally with

17

vastly increased formal education. All evidence attests to the rapid differentiation of persons breaking loose from the bounds of peasant existence. Fear of intellectual constrictions by the mass media and the culture has caused more persons to explore ever greater implications within our culture, each developing his private and unique view of it. Tolerance of all behavior, including indifference to it, becomes endemic. Insofar as a general population grows sophisticated it loses homogeneity; it is more free in its opinions and uses them more freely. Yet it is not thereby any less interdependent since the very multiplication of views within it and each member's more highly delineated personality (as I define personality) make each dependent upon a larger number of others, similarly specialized in outlook, in order to cross-check his views and orient himself amidst a richly various existence.

This obvious development exactly reverses eighteenth and nineteenth century expectations of so-called free discussion and expression. Whereas an eighteenth century gentleman scholar could plausibly anticipate that popular education would reduce the variety of local village customs, superstitions, prejudices—and that Reason applied to Nature would banish ignorance, leaving a residue of common enlightenment—enlightenment turns out to be not some body of opinion self-evidently true for everyone but an expansion of individual insights and specialization of knowledge; the diversity of interpretations of enlightenment were undreamed of even by the most ardent apostle of "civilized progress." Whereas it was supposed that "progress" would allow every enlightened individual to work his way in the world more easily and unaided, the reverse is true. Diversity and specialization make us more interdependent than before; the failure to understand this (in place of common interests and general will) explains why nineteenth century advocates of personal "liberty" did not realize a corresponding

18

need to integrate and govern diversity. If our absolute differences of endowment and condition were reshaped to make us alike, we would destroy the viability of community without which we perish. Instead, we depend upon social systems for our wants, of which we are prisoners, and cannot discard but only modify them despite our frustrations. We must fit ourselves to these systems, not having found among us a common will. Rather, diversity and specialization ever multiply while concomitantly does our interdependence.

The only resolution of these dilemmas is social organization of such a character that no ordinary citizen is required to judge another's function or contribution to society or required to develop a social philosophy of desirable community behavior, or to be responsible for his own education and direction. Instead, those who can integrate and manage talents must advise each citizen and hold him liable for following their advice. In short, no one should have to fit himself to a social system any more than is necessary; nor can he know how much or little is required except if he is told. This obvious resolution would not have taken so long to develop if the contrary had not been supposed since John Locke's time. The contrary is that every citizen's freedom consists in his knowing his own interests and in acting on them, as if to preserve his integrity were to require his omniscience, which decidedly none possesses.

At the same time these reflections restrict desirable social systems to those which appear potentially tyrannical, since whoever governs, by advising citizens of their obligations, is no less individual and idiosyncratic than other members of the community. The excuse for government does not arise, however, out of anyone's accidental possession of talents for governing but out of our need for government due to our diversity-and-interdependence, whether or not anyone is capable of fulfilling that need. It is therefore possible that no one in a community can be a wise ruler; such an event would in no way alter the need for someone to rule. Proportionally as a ruler or his assistants are poor advisors, or fail to understand the dilemma which I have been describing, all suffer. To counter this possibility, civic responsibility is urged upon everyone throughout the world. The goal is that people judge one another as if they understood as well as their governors how to integrate and manage everyone's talents; that they advise and hold each other liable for what they advise; and that they possess reasons justifying their acts. It does not matter whether there be constitutional arrangements for accomplishing these aims or how poorly they work or how difficult it is to perfect them. Even revolution would be desirable if only it were clear whether judging each other and, thus, ruling ourselves is desirable. Some means might always be found to translate those judgments for our common use.

Interdependence itself requires immediate judgments of how heavily we lean upon each other, of whether we have any choice but trusting one another. In this sense there is no problem of our self-government; it exists inherently within and through the web of our interactions. But it is another matter whether we can reach behind the range of these relationships, as it were, to undo others' judgments, reorder their relationships, and tyrannize over others as I have suggested that governors do. It should be taken seriously whether advising others does not engender greater examination and knowledge of the self and of all things affecting human welfare than any other act within a society. Were there a common will rationally justifying our advice, or less diversity of opinions on matters unknown by many but important to us all, advice to one another could stand securely on a foundation of limited insights impervious to anyone's realizing their tyranny. But such limited insights are not now possible, and probably never were; was there ever a community so narrow in outlook that no one understood more than his fellows but everyone could as easily advise and be advised as could anyone else? Is not seeking and training oneself to judge others an extension of the talents of parenthood or of care for neighbors' affairs? And if some persons have much of such talent, they will all the more hesitate to tyrannize over others because of experience with their own fallibilities. If some know a great deal about anything they will all the more hesitate to challenge others' knowledge because they realize how much others may understand which they do not.

It follows that all who would be governors advising everyone else cannot have such hesitancies, else they cannot rule. Likewise all who actually govern must be tyrannical unconsciously, out of insensitivity and ignorance, from which all must suffer. Social systems, which arbitrarily demand that ordinary people incapable of ruling must rule, are worthless. Thus civic responsibility is impossible and the blame for what rulers do is falsely laid upon the population at large. A general population is too various, inclusive of the wise and the ignorant, the aware and the unaware, to be its own leader. Rulers alone can be held responsible for what they do. We possess rulers for more reasons than I have yet developed; but even now it can be seen that interdependence implies the necessity for integration and for management and that human populations are too various for everyone collectively to rule. Therefore a few rule, and the rest are advised of their roles in the social system, whatever those be. And because of these circumstances, because there is no feasible way around them, rulers arrogate to themselves vast powers, and become autocratic, tyrannical. The question, then, is what can be done about it.

III.

REALITIES OF POPULAR GOVERNMENT

We come into the world subject to whatever our parents impose upon us. Likewise we grow up within a culture that ill-fits our individual situations from moment to moment. Every culture has been a system of behavior differently perceived by each member and therefore perceived in some degree differently by the rulers than by the ruled. And all this is done largely without governors realizing their arbitrariness and largely despite anyone's protest or rebellion. Regardless of whether the macrocosmic explanation of animate social survival on this planet is survival through conflict, the microcosmic explanation of individual behavior is our submission to and victimization by the social system within which we were born.

Why need societies be ruled so ruthlessly? One reason was given above: sensitive and gentle persons would never attempt to rule. A second reason is organizational. In a society of persons needing to aid and supply one another there must be social organization, or each will go off in his own direction and cooperate with others only amidst interminable discussion and debate, trial and error. Organization can be simple or complex. If each tries to arrange with every other how their mutual work shall dovetail, organization is maximally complex. Each must interact with every other until each knows what every other has decided and can reconcile his own decisions with those of the rest. Such a feat demands forbearance, self-discipline, and selflessness beyond anything dreamed of by the most naive poets. A more simple organization is essential. The most simple is to have a single boss or very small committee decide for and direct everyone else. Elaborations upon this form of government are everywhere familiar; none diverges very far from the basic model of a boss with final authority over all citizens. The heads of all contemporary nation states are given such wide discretion over ultimate decisions that so-called limited governments and so-called dictatorships differ only slightly. It must then be concluded either that governments are inherently authoritarian, or potentially so—or else that this view of government is incomplete.

We find that it is incomplete by asking whether millions of ruled obey a few rulers at the cost of self-respect and of freedom to act as they like, merely for the sake of social efficiency. The answer is clear. Even after someone among a crowd of isolated persons conceives how they may cooperate, and leads them, his instructions are fruitless without nearly everyone's understanding and willing response. No boss can put into the minds of the bossed more than indications of what each should do; each must reconcile some minimal enthusiasm for the project with what he will allow himself to do, as determined by his integrity, his pride, and his capacity for enjoyment or endurance. These requirements being met, a supportive environment is achieved through his having been assigned a role and function, and through the work of still others who, since his childhood, enculturated him to respond. Otherwise attempts to work together will seem unnatural, forced; a situation to be escaped rather than pursued. Even slaves have had to find some way of consenting to their condition before slave economies could be viable. Social organization necessitates some one to elicit consent but also the giving of consent. Likewise dissatisfaction and ennui among the bossed frustrates anything that a boss may wish. Dictation in itself is a barren exercise of wasted breath. Failure of the ruled to make a virtue of necessity, to find dignity and satisfaction in serving as much

24

as in being served, dooms any cooperative enterprise. Social organization must transcend mere efficiency and utility by engendering positive responses. Otherwise the whole fabric of societal intercourse shreds away. But certainly none of this happens spontaneously, as many seem to suppose. All earliest explanations of the origin of human association consistently affirmed the presence of an initial law-giver, a single genius at social mobilization. Upon this assumption there must have been a first ruler prior to any first community. He conceived and constructed it by commanding people to associate in given ways. Thereupon arose the need of a supportive environment for subsequent cooperation, a process of mutual reinforcement between satisfactions and their occasions.

The ability to find satisfaction in social cooperation, to contribute to enterprises under another's direction, lies within each person's varying capacity for self-development. The greater part of consent to being bossed is not legitimized by labor contracts or by the acts of public office-holders, but by the capacities of workers or citizens to open themselves to experience, to make something good of their days. This insight alters and helps to complete the one-sided view that dictation by a boss creates slaves of everyone else. Instead, a boss' dictation accomplishes nothing without others' positive willingness to support what the boss commands. Likewise lack of positive satisfaction constitutes a veto, even if unintended and unconscious, upon the boss' rule—a veto which no boss may be able to counter, since if the bossed do not have within them any power of response, there is nothing for any boss to elicit. The point is crucial for a model of fallible and unequally talented persons. The idea of social organization and of founding particular polities no doubt arises in the mind of some single individual, but its implementation always depends on the proportion of members of that organization with capacity for positive response. Only in this way can we explain the persistence and accomplishments of slave economies, of autocratic rule, of all those forms of government which eighteenth century democratic theory declared unworkable.

Yet unless there be some way to assess the direction and force of this supportive social environment, it can be greatly misunderstood and thereby enterprises can fail. The most obvious means for making such an assessment is for rulers to put an ear to the ground and feel out the temper of people's morale. This necessity has been interpreted to imply the presence of inherent rights of people to be heard and heeded. There can be no quarrel with anyone's assuming that he has such rights or with his assertion of them whenever rulers are prudent enough to listen. But rights of any sort are only effective as they are acknowledged by those against whom they are asserted. Rights enacted into law are reminders of people's claims for attention and of others' intent to respect such claims. The more serious and necessitous aspect of the relationship of leaders and led, or of one social group's behavior toward another, is that no one should assume another's willingness to cooperate. There are no easy explanations of human moods whether between spouses, among a family, or more broadly among groups and a population as a whole; but everyone from moment to moment senses the clear presence or absence of others' willingness to respond one way or another, and this constitutes a basic ingredient (along with someone to lead such willingness toward some end) for any social achievement. Yet morale does not in itself initiate anything; it responds. The led cannot advise their leader how to organize work or what goals to seek; they can only reveal how much or little satisfaction they have chosen, or been able, to find in what they have been asked to do. It is precisely here where nineteenth century political theory assumed too much. That citizens must be motivated for any polity to exist cannot imply that they are also capable or anxious to decide in what directions their motivation should lead them, and consequently what policies their rulers should pursue. On the other hand the citizenry's hesitations, dissatisfactions, and the whole complex of their emotional and intellectual self-confidence must limit every ruler's freedom of action. The myth that the led can lead their leaders and the myth that leaders must wait upon direction from their followers are imaginative projections of a ruler's necessary dependence upon citizens' morale and their capacity to respond positively toward their rulers.

Such imaginative projections are common. They arise from people's need to understand complex phenomena in more simple ways. Opposite the myth of democratic self-government is the myth of ability to coerce obedience. No leader of more than a handful of persons can physically enforce his will upon them. He must use police, military forces, or a host of persons who agree with what he intends or he becomes a ridiculous figure talking to himself alone. And as for those whom police coerce, either they must agree to be coerced or civil war results and there are two polities instead of one. Finally, even in civil or international war, all enemies must share some understanding that there is a war going on, or no conflict is possible and no peace negotiable. This is not to write off conflict as a friendly game but to ask how it is that humans, who never perceive alike what are purportedly the same events, nevertheless achieve limited consensus even when opposed.

Consensus is achieved by generalizing what would only confuse everyone if it were specified, and by everyone's abiding willingness and often strong desire to think well of what each finds himself doing. It is well known that the less a leader argues in public, the more he states opinions as if there were no alternatives, the more he assumes agreement by his listeners, the more readily people believe him, obey him, and (in elections) vote for him. When war is declared, opposing heads of state only confuse each other if the issue is made more complex than merely denial of the other ruler's righteousness. What we call consensus does not arise from any spontaneous combustion of historical forces but from our needs for ego-reinforcement— even when people are not required to decide anything but only to go along. This extraordinary phenomenon does not modify individuality and personality but softens the outlines of what people perceive and permits obedience under conditions that do not challenge or affect self-awareness; people lose themselves in obedience, reclaim themselves in diversity of outlook.

Apparent self-government by all is possible in these circumstances but depends upon the relinquishment of self-government by each for government by someone else. What has been taken as a "people's will" is actually their consent to be ruled. We have only short lives, limited energies. That evil is done is undeniable; why it happens without greater protest or awareness has been partially explained. The world is fantastically imperfect. Yet what I have claimed—the necessity for organization of work by a boss, the need for positive response to his demands, the boss' incapacity to enforce compliance physically, and yet people's willingness to think well of what they find themselves doing—is not an unhappy complex of conditions for political rule. Humans would have to be very different creatures were anything else at all feasible. For this reason political reform traditionally has called for a "new Soviet man" or relied upon a "New World" America to "free" people from "old ways." New men may arise but as they do, new and presently unimaginable means of governing must be found. It is possible that if someday leaders fail to elicit consensus as heretofore, a vast inversion of matters political would have to take place whereby at least part of a population would act autonomously, without direct political guidance. This last sentence paints a pretty picture of freedom from constraint but also freedom from involvement or interdependence. It resembles that nineteenth century notion of anarchic "higher living" with which rootless aristocrats and pretenders to intellectual exclusiveness regaled their imaginations. At the other extreme, it is possible that if consensus were gradually to involve more than willingness to go along, were to awaken people's creative energies for drawing close to one another, clinging to each other, insisting not just on agreement but that they give one another their hearts, then government might become an Inquisition or another Calvinist Geneva. Again, the world is fantastically imperfect but at least malleable; it is structured despite its indefinite measurements, though untidy despite political order. For this reason of general social inefficiency the conditions of political rule persist universally regardless of forms of government, peace or war, means of production, styles of artistic representation, the blandishments of new sciences or of private creeds. So long as a culture fits individual desires poorly, people must either understand some good in it or rebel. Revolutions are not inherently foolish since they have brought many changes now enjoyed. The problem is to know what would perfect our imperfection.

People's capacities for positive response to a ruler's demands plus the consensus resulting from people's willingness to believe well of what they are doing are undoubtedly the root and ground of political morality. Because here the care of the community is most tangibly performed. The demos, the people, meet themselves through a leader's management of relationships already existing among them but directionless until he appears to "discover" their common intention. A leader brings the same order to a group or a nation through his suggestions and style of behavior that a kindergarten teacher brings to children. I am not saying that morality, even political morality, consists in orderliness but that morality involves the good of everyone rather than merely of one person here, another there; otherwise my good at someone else's expense would be a moral outcome of any conflict. Morality involves all parties to an encounter;

it must embrace everyone. This happens only through the agency of a polity. Yet a polity's leadership may be unaware of the nature of morality and certainly is far from capable of knowing everyone's good, and in any case is inherently dictatorial and self-righteous. But that does not alter the fact that only through the working out of a polity's continued existence can people achieve whatever good is possible, however little that may be. Kindergarten children survive the worst leadership and often develop—by obscure processes, perhaps more chemical than intellectual—new convictions of their own never held by anyone near them. But it makes a great difference whether a child undergoes this experience with other children in some orderly, supportive environment or alone at his mother's knee. With other children he suffers rejection or learns the joys of selfish dominance (unless he be sensitive enough to invent some wider role) while alone he learns only self-pity. Rejection or selfishness at least are uncomfortable enough to stimulate a search for alternatives which self-pity would only decline in favor of standing in a corner. A kindergarten teacher cannot tend all her charges at every moment and therefore in the end, like other leaders, opts for peace among them at almost any cost. In the end she teaches them to go along with her ideas for the day or hour; she politicizes them in the sense that political regimes are said to be "good" in proportion to their social stability and the absence of any, except a loyal, opposition. The care of a kindergarten community like the care of larger polities is first expressed in the peace of the realm. This is so whether constitutionally a ruler is called upon to represent a popular will (within Soviet or other theories of general welfare and public interest government) or to represent in himself the guardianship of a tribe or an empire.

The responsibility for the consequences of his rule is the ruler's, and evasion of that responsibility by pretending that he follows only popular initiative or bends to popular inertia is a peculiar self-deception of contemporary elected leaders and without parallel in previous political cultures. Whether the evasion can be called immoral, because it ignores the grounds of political morality, is at least arguable; democracy in the sense of everyone's collective instruction of a ruler is, anyway, impossible. What is left is not people's restrictions upon rulers but how far rulers can be expected to understand their role. Their failures corrode their own self-confidence as well as the community as a whole. The good or evil of their acts is not something arbitrarily determinable by some philosopher sitting on a hill outside the polity; it can be judged only by the consequences of those unavoidable conditions surrounding implementation of the political function. The rough shape of those conditions has already been sketched; particularities follow. They have been universal conditions as far as human history has advanced; yet history is never closed.

IV.

THE INCLUSIVE POLITY

It has been shown that a community subsists both upon leadership and its members' positive response. Leadership need not be by a single person; committees and boards may do quite as well as single leaders but even here one person in the committee must be given authority to regulate debate. No matter how near or far apart are members of a committee, how compliant or cooperative, they require leadership just as greatly and for the same reason as any other group. The structure of societies has been compared to that of an onion whose each successive skin supports or leads the next outer one, relying for its support upon the next inner one. But that image of a total society fails to account for the individuals composing each layer who, though said to be members of the same social class or generation, differ among themselves as much or more than do classes or generations. In order, then, that any group or committee has common ground for discussion, a single person among them must again take the lead by preparing a study of all rational choices of action and reporting these to members before they meet. Members may then amend that report to include additional choices or delete others before debating whether to act upon any of them. If their decision is not unanimous, any minorities must still support the majority or the committee dissolves into factions. Unity, singleness in the result, is unavoidable. The same is true for a total population whenever minorities find it difficult to tolerate or adjust to majority behavior, and the same phenomenon explains the present disunity among nation states when any state fails to tolerate or adjust to any other despite lack of agreement to act by majority decision.

Two and only two conceivable consequences follow from inability of persons or governments to tolerate or adjust to one another. The first is that they go their separate ways, avoiding and ignoring each other. The second is that one or many seek to dominate and rule over those with whom they cannot agree, much as a leader commands his followers. Going their separate ways is generally impractical. The exception arises when a majority is so great that the refusal of a minority to cooperate barely detracts from the supportive social environment maintaining the community; care of that community does not require adjustment to the minority. Under this condition alone can persons or governments go their own ways; under all other conditions the community will be destroyed and everyone else's activities impaired if not totally frustrated. As minorities become a larger proportion of the whole, it matters more and more that they submit to majority rule in the sense described above. It has often been noted that the corollary of viable dictation is the dictator's care of those submitting to him, as argued in the previous chapter. All this is only to say that when the conditions of the first alternative are not present, the second alternative automatically arises.

The second alternative, seeking to dominate and rule over those who disagree with us, has been widely interpreted as providing opportunity to eliminate through some sort of open discussion the less desirable courses of behavior. It is a hopeful suggestion. But it rests upon a host of new conditions. It assumes that those involved have agreed how to discuss, and what shall constitute rational or otherwise insightful argument, which in turn means agreement upon what is admissible evidence. It also assumes that the breadth and depth of evidence will encompass at least the more desirable alternatives and that these will be affirmed. Finally it assumes that affirmation will engender consent to act. Such assumptions are wholly gratuitous among a population of deficient persons unless they be enculturated to know what they are doing, agree upon what is admissible, be satisfied that it is comprehensive enough to have included desirable alternatives, and be prepared to recognize these and to consent in their undertaking. In short, any probability that we can dominate and rule over those who disagree with us presupposes a common culture. What is true and false must already have been decided, and there must be willingness to act in accordance with relative weights of value placed upon them. We are not creatures of unbounded insight able to balance any number of variables against each other and calculate their sum. Our interdependence includes reliance upon each other's ideas, and their range and number cannot be too great.

Where no common culture exists are we then doomed to perpetual struggle? It has already been argued that a community may embrace mutual enemies. But need all enemies be drawn by the experience of interacting with each other into recognition of each other's ways, and thus into some mutual understanding that eventually must make them one community? It is likely or there is no explanation for survival of the human race; mutual suicide would long ago have been accomplished. It becomes clear that any conflict however unstructured takes on the character of a game with rules for its conduct. These may not at first be realized. Action against an enemy whether in war or any other situation (a family quarrel, a bitter debate) draws us closer to him and he to us by the mere fact of having to grapple with his presence, with what he may do to us. And then suppose that we defeat him: can he be ignored, left to shift for himself? Could we in defeat shift for ourselves? It has never been so, however much this happy picture of having no responsibility for our acts may appeal to us in the midst of competition. Victorious communities have enslaved their opponents only to discover the cost of keeping them; defeated peoples have had to cooperate with their victors; a family is never rid of its most obnoxious members. A zero-sum game in which one actor destroys another and is never bothered by him again is a misapplication to animate behavior of games of chance played with inanimate objects. A zero-sum game between humans is not properly a game of any sort but a pact by which neither actor is willing or able to consider any consequences beyond destruction for its own sake; as such, it is wholly unrealistic.

The experience of personal combat leaves indelible impressions known only by those who have wounded another and watched him die. This experience is denied leaders who command millions of such acts, and seems to require imagination beyond many leaders' capacities. The world is therefore constantly threatened by the inability of leaders to care for their own communities or to realize themselves within a community including those whom they lead and those whom they attack. But the consequence is clear. Insofar as individuals destroy each other and insofar as communities are torn apart by civil war, the supportive environment (the sole means by which interdependent humans can survive) is endangered and possibly ended for all time. Since leaders lead and few other citizens can, the result is the constant vulnerability of citizens to their leaders' misapprehension of the conditions within which politics must be conducted.

It has already been argued that citizens cannot advise rulers what to do or how to do it. They can only respond to conditions over which they have no more control than that allowed by what each can do for others whom he influences. Citizens are characteristically led into serving their rulers and abiding by their procedures as in the case of military service against members of other polities similarly persuaded by their rulers. The citizen acquiesces or rebels. Rebellion may be justified but it requires new leaders opposed to the established leaders, and also a known game of rebellion which preserves the community. There is no escape from the conclusion that leaders of all factions are responsible for preserving the community even if that community embraces the whole human race.

A first step in the direction of preserving the race might be to outlaw weapons of mass destruction because the consent of those masses to their own destruction could never be obtained, even in the sense that conscripted men consent to being drafted. Yet lesser weapons are easily constructed. Their use against governments or other citizens is at all times a possibility. The picture at once comes to mind of an all-seeing dictatorship which searches every cranny for evidence of arms manufacture and punishes anyone found violating a law against possession of weapons. It is not a pretty picture. But something of the sort may have to be done until the habits of easy and irresponsible violence now prevalent (and encouraged in our mass media) are superseded by more pacifist inclinations. The subtleties and complexities of individual cases are nearly infinite and will never be reduced to any formula. Special courts and appropriate measures for keeping the peace must forever be perfected and altered to meet the intellectual-psychological expectations of each time and place.

What can be said more generally is that participation in repressive activities should always be voluntary, never enforced through a draft of young persons. Would not voluntary recruitment make large scale international war impossible? At this moment it could be true. But no one dare suppose that for centuries to come there will not be leaders able to mobilize military crusades. Making participation in war voluntary will not end wars, but right now it would vastly reduce the capability of governments to threaten one another. Perhaps a portion of the earth should be set aside for unlimited combat among those voluntarily desiring to live outside the bounds of any community. The Amazon basin could be walled about; no one entering could ask protection or aid while within those walls; occurrences there would never be inquired into and few would be expected to return. Such a fanciful arena for unhindered violence may someday serve the purpose of dramatizing the cost to persons of reentering what Hobbes called the State of Nature.

Meanwhile any force used to suppress warfare must answer the complaints of anti-militarists that the mere presence of armies and of everything needed to support them threatens the security of the general public. Lives and fortunes are constantly endangered by the possibility of unexpected use of military force or arbitrary decisions by political or military officers to avoid or intensify military action. The only solution is the imposition by all political regimes, mutually and collectively, of rules for the conduct of violence. There would be slight sense in any rules for conducting violence which did not assure everyone of the opportunity to assess the cost of violence beforehand, to contract, as it were, for potential injuries in return for potential gains. Participants would then be able to renegotiate that contract at given costs whenever the battle went against them, to opt out as readily as opt in. Such rules of warfare are no invention of mine; to some degree they have always existed. Their peculiar difficulty is that rules can be effective only with consent of the vast majority of those affected, which today is the world's population. Even if all governments agree upon some enforceable code, the necessity for engineering consent of the governed would tempt each government to make that consent a clever device for discerning potential enemies. Mere admission that there are potential enemies would raise distrust among popular majorities in one polity toward popular majorities in another. The present impasse in international relations is due at least as much to this problem of obtaining consent as to the political shortsightedness of heads of state. Any world-wide code of conduct however generous and well conceived would necessarily require forbearance and self-discipline, for sacrifices would always seem unequal. Minorities will be short-changed. Adjudication of grievances still allows resentments to carry over into political action by small or large minorities against the peace of the rest of the globe. The opposite case can also exist whenever a majority of the world population agrees to distrust some portion of its own number not of the same color or creed; that majority is then open to being led by anyone pretending to seek peace through enlisting parts of the world population against other parts. Such is a simple description of the contemporary international system.

All of these considerations are reducible to one political model. It is that exclusion of anyone from a polity endangers everyone else. This is an unwieldy model because it supposes that each in some way can be reconciled to all others. It is difficult to apply even in families where children await the day when they will escape their parents' supervision and temperaments. But its logic is undeniable. The argument for social interdependence leads directly to the conclusion that, even if a dissident social remnant withdraws into some other place, it remains entangled with its former community to the extent that there are conscious enmities. But if some withdraw so far out of sight, or are so self-sufficient, that they have no dealings with anyone else, then certainly there is no longer a case of exclusion but of two separate worlds unknown to each other.

Yet there must be acts for which people can be imprisoned, either to secure their own good or to protect the rest. If allowed loose in the world they might influence others and gradually corrupt the polity. When rulers of some part of a polity are evil, though their followers be innocent (of whatever crimes or corruptive doctrines we may imagine), exclusion of those rulers and all who innocently follow them might save the rest of humanity from their machinations. There may not be time to permit conflict among rulers or among followers to engender the sense of community that would water down their evil. Regicide is an obvious answer, but it merely makes martyrs. Similarly, any notorious exclusion of whole peoples can only make all men curious to meet them or anxious to experiment with the ideas or acts that were the cause of that people's exclusion. Finally it has always been true that criminals are heroes just because they defy their betters, are not fit to be associated with, and thereby intrigue both all idealistic young men and cynical old men to learn about them, repeat their words, and retell their acts.

If no one can be profitably excluded, if all wars and incarcerations defeat the ends that presumably they serve, and if the means used to gain those abortive ends are terrible in themselves—is viable politics reduced to persuading everyone that he must care for his neighbor, whoever he be? That answer has already been suggested by the discussion of minority submission to majority rule and majority care for minority interests. It is illustrated in the history of political parties for the last hundred years. These parties were founded by a few leaders having particular interests which they wished endorsed by a sufficient number of others either to win an election (and so be able to dictate as they desired) or to lead a minority whom majority leaders would have to heed. Yet whenever a number of parties sought irreconcilable interests, no government of the whole community was possible. In those cases either no single party could dominate the rest or, even if it could, the irreconcilability of the others' interests prevented the dominant party from caring for them. As a result those with excluded interests were forced to consider civil war. Historically, the only solution has been that leaders of all political movements within any nation consult together, and decide what range of interests they might all support despite disagreement on this and that detail. Rather than a free-for-all confrontation, inherent rules emerge in any political game. The first of these is that none shall be excluded from a common game but that all shall agree how far each may deviate from some central core of reconcilable issues. Those who cannot enter this consensus must be brought into it. Here is the heart of viable political existence.

The means to this end are many and difficult. It is extraordinarily desirable that all potential leaders in any polity attend the same or similar schools, or at least meet each other under school-like conditions where ideas and diverse experiences are intimately discussed. A political culture in which leaders' privacy is seldom or diffidently invaded must necessarily impede accommodation because no leader can be certain what another means; he is unfamiliar with another's thoughts and peculiar ways of expression. The world is a large place but anything done within it must be managed by individual persons working together; no matter how large a government, only a few can arrange any particular action and, in the course of those arrangements, each individual who is party to them counts enormously in the result. His temperament, his knowledge of the others, their mutual trust or distrust: these are everything. No investment of political resources is worth so much as having potential political leaders share a part of each other's lives before they come to office. It is therefore obvious that the greatest lack in contemporary world politics is the often total unfamiliarity of rulers and chief officials with one another. This lack provides greater potentiality for conflict and world civil war than lacks of formal organization, of disarmament, or of sophistication about the boundaries of political action.

None of the foregoing suggests that viable politics can be undertaken only within an elite isolated from the rest of humanity. Although leaders cannot feasibly rule without limiting their interests to whatever consensus excludes none of the other leaders, a vast array of interests outside that consensus must continually lie in wait to embarrass and ambush the whole political game that the established leaders are trying to play. Such is the daily fact of political existence. Governing means excluding some alternatives in favor of others, even while the object of governing is the care of a total community's potentialities for what is excluded as well as for that already included. But is this an argument for tolerating tyranny? Any program can be justified by appealing to the impossibility of its being all-inclusive. The short answer is that governors must not suppress ideas or they martyrize them; governors must encourage the venting of all dissidence until the vast variety of prejudices, idiosyncrasies, and blindnesses have been absorbed within the existing political consensus. That I can be sanguine about this process is not due to aloofness from partisan emotion; rather it is due to recognition that any political consensus imposed by established leaders must necessarily have been widely disseminated and have largely formed everyone's political awareness, and thus be nearly impervious to fatal attack.

Yet there remains the problem that a world political elite might impose not an innocuous political consensus but one so shortsighted as to endanger further human existence. Other judgments than those which are already well accepted or which are supported by distinguished men are likely to shape each successive future decade. How are these to penetrate the consciousness of a world elite? Is there greater probability that a given unconventional view is more easily accepted by a very large number of small, isolated, and provincially minded elites —or by a large, secure, and therefore tolerant elite? Certainly in the case of industrial enterprises, innovation has been more continuous and profound the larger the enterprise and the less it has had to conserve resources to meet competition; likewise a single community newspaper more easily publishes a variety of news than several who compete to attract the largest number of purely conventional readers. In every federal system of government it is the national government which, because of its size, resources, and superior jurisdiction, more easily tolerates deviation and admits innovation than the provincial or state governments federated with it.

The argument has been for a single polity either very loosely constructed, as among two armies pitted against each other, or closely knit, as among rival political parties or the governments of a federal system. But a community of opponents is hardly as secure as one of merely dominant factions unavoidably caring for the interests of minorities. In the first case there develops respect between enemies, in the other there develops tolerance and even affection for those whom no one need fear. Yet none of this is automatic or spontaneous. The players must monitor themselves and each other. In cases of a clearly dominant faction, the political game can be monitored by the use of boards and commissions to regulate the interplay of lesser factions. Where there is no dominant faction but an uneasy alliance of several, or lack of any formal association among fully sovereign governments, each faction must seek the other's sanction for policies mutually affecting one another. Unilateral behavior is rare. International diplomacy is no more than seeking other nations' sanction, whether wisely for mutual gain or foolishly for a selfish one which will certainly be returned in kind. The same good and ill effects are just as apparent among legally co-equal branches of a government constructed on the principle of separation of powers as they are among independent sovereign nations. Institutionalized or not, partners in any enterprise must acknowledge one another's claims or, unaware that they are partners, must suffer the longer and more painful discovery that as enemies they will gradually be drawn together within a single community.

This longer and more painful process leaves the general

population waiting for politicians to learn their craft. Why, then, cannot representatives of the people, properly elected and authorized as a legislature to sanction the behavior of government leaders, umpire the political game in the people's interests? A host of questions arise. Is there an interest of the people separate from what government leaders say is their interest? For a government to exist, its leaders must already have enculturated sanction of their rule. That sanction may include the concept of loyal opposition, developing from interests separate from the government's. Yet if separateness of interest can frustrate government, no government would enculturate sanction of it. Therefore, whatever a representative of the people (himself becoming thereby a part of the government) "discovers" to be the people's interest, cannot be used to monitor government unless it is compatible with what government has already enculturated. Popular legislatures are therefore redundant; they only reinforce what already has been politically established. In short, unless everyone could be his own leader and not need government, from what wellspring of knowledgeable decision-making can anyone instruct his representative? That question has generally been answered by supposing that people cannot instruct their representatives, but that representatives must intuit what people would wish if people could know what their representatives know. Yet such virtual representation is quite as actual in the case of non-legislative branches of government, and so there is no need to erect against those branches any legislature at all. This strategy of representation is already employed through popular election of heads of state; but then why should not citizen interest be identically expressed through both a chief executive and a legislature (elected by the same public) so that small difference of opinion would exist between them? This has never happened, and I am forced to conclude that there are as many public interests as there are leaders who conceive them.

44

The Inclusive Polity

Does this conclusion amount to cruel and unusual punishment of the general public? It would certainly be so if the general populace were the sole and true community while leaders were outside it. That often enough was an eighteenth century conclusion due to the social distance between aristocrats and the rest. But in fact leaders and led are of one community in which everyone contributes something, governors no less than others. There emerges an inherent design bounding political action. The moral implicit in this design is that none can viably be excluded from a polity even while few can rule. Polities are interdependencies of persons, and their boundaries are reached only where interdependence ceases, but they are not thereby collective minds. They have no will, only leaders who in our time are said to represent such a non-existent will. Leadership must largely monitor itself even at the risk that, if it does not, it will not gain a positive response from the led, and will thus be powerless. Popular representation was originally conceived to fulfill an entirely different model than the one here proposed. That model was not of an entire population, some leaders, some led; it was a model of leaders only, self-reliant and well informed heads of households who were to decide public policy. Not until the nineteenth century, was everyone else supposed to have become like these leaders, though not of them, and thus in a position to instruct their fellows-become-legislators. And meanwhile their fellows-become-legislators no longer were trained in or familiar with public management or in a position to lead; they could only pretend to be led by their constituents. The boundaries of political action are confused whenever the led attempt to lead, or those representing them pretend to be led. Yet for all these difficulties, legislatures serve the function of symbolizing something greater than themselves which they cannot be—a people's individual and specific responses to leadership. Those responses are felt throughout a polity and are the substance of everyday existence. Some are heard, some not, but if any are excluded from being heard (as if in any other game the losers were excluded from ever playing again) or if, in being heard, they exclude themselves from the benefits of the supportive social environment, then those excluded have no interest in maintaining or saving the community. Their loss of hope can only ensure their determination to destroy everyone else. It follows that no one should be left outside the society lest their absolute alienation fail to elicit compassion from their fellows. The fault is clear but the cure cannot await general enlightenment; we do not live long enough to learn from our mistakes.

The problem is returned to political leaders. It becomes the first order of business to educate leaders in their responsibility for avoiding civil war within a world polity. The education of princes was once the chief subject of political philosophy because it was always realized, prior to the last few hundred years, that care of the community lies first with princes and secondly with citizens, due to all the reasons developed above. Yet these arguments have never impressed princes either in their youth under competent tutors or today in schools and universities. For all the primacy of princes' powers of initiative and command, and for all their awareness of those powers, princes are seldom sufficiently humbled by that awareness to study seriously how to be intelligent rulers, as artists study techniques and visions of previous artists, or physicians study the human body. Machiavelli was a most able civil servant and ambassador who constantly studied records of his craft, but his masters largely ignored his advice. The same phenomenon is everywhere apparent today.

V.

LEADERS, LAWS, AND JUSTICE

It is entirely plausible that genius consists in the ability simultaneously to weigh a large number of factors against each other, bearing their relationships in mind, and resolve their opposition without prejudice to any variable. But that is not an ordinary talent. The ordinary person is aware of at least some parts of any problem, and is not likely to find other people any better informed although their information will concern other parts of that same problem, loosely joined and connected with his. From this circumstance arises the popular belief that if a number of people put their heads together, their united information will issue in a collective judgment superior to any decision that each could make alone. Yet this belief is seldom if ever demonstrated because no ordinary person can reconcile within himself the sum of what he knew before and what he now hears from others; few can make up their minds and so wait for someone else to propose some course of action resolving doubts which each still harbors but would prefer to put aside at least to settle the matter. That "someone else" becomes a leader. He is hardly ever an ordinary person among the rest even if no one till this moment recognizes his leadership. His private vision of what the rest are discussing impels him to arouse them from their blindness and lethargy. His judgment is mistaken, of course, since the rest are more aware than he of many concerns lying at cross purposes to his own and resolvable only by ignoring some or exaggerating others. But the leader's vision is never so complex. He sees it all from his point of view.

He has few if any doubts. Equivocation is not in his makeup. He is one of those few who have no difficulty making up their minds; he may almost be said not to perceive choices between courses of action but, as if squinting with one eye, to grasp what has to be done and direct the rest. If they balk or hang back, he spurs them on with more vivid images embodying what either from the beginning, or now under the influence of his own eloquence, appears to him without rebuttal. He makes an invaluable contribution because without his fervor nothing in particular might ever be done; and at the same time he endangers everyone's welfare by shutting off potential gains from other courses. Shakespeare described it—to be or not to be. Without decision there cannot be anything, and with it all may be lost.

Artists behave similarly but with a significant difference. Whereas Hamlet was an ordinary mortal unable to choose, and political leaders are extraordinary in being able to perceive no alternative than that which impells them to seize leadership, an artist purposely exaggerates, foreshortens, dramatizes in order to reveal through simplification first one aspect, then another of what he perceives. Unlike the politican he must originally have perceived far more than what he presents or else what he presents in a foreshortened, simplified form would not readily be recognized as something more than the few strokes of a lithographer's pencil. Such is equally the art of a social scientist's analytic model, a natural scientist's theory, an architect's design. The very purpose of arts of every sort is to isolate some discrete aspect of total reality for study or specialized presentation in order that it be understood without intrusion by the rest of reality. The multiplication of arts and sciences accounts for our greater skill at dealing with discrete problems. But the ordinary citizen and his leaders are in quite a different situation (as are artists and scientists when not practicing their professions). Living together, we cannot isolate ourselves from one another or deal only with some discrete aspect of another's interaction with us, and become irresponsible toward the remainder. Total reality is forever with us even though often out of focus,. dim, and difficult to take in at a glance; for this reason we find ourselves unable to choose one course of action over another. Therefore we need leaders. But for all a leader's decisiveness it is the worst error to suppose that his judgments are at all reliable, for he is inevitably unaware of the whole of reality with which the rest of us must live (which nevertheless he supposes to be embodied within his own one-eyed vision). Hopefully those closest to him will realize this deficiency and consequently be prepared to criticize him or support another leader in his place—whereas easy criticism of artistic or scientific works is precluded by their neatness of design and discriminating conclusiveness.

It is a shocking fact that so many decisions beyond the wisest man's capability are daily brought for final and nearly irrevocable decision to the heads of state of so-called democracies as well as so-called dictatorships. It is shocking because without question none of their decisions can have any effect unless the world's citizenry positively responds by carrying out such decisions. And the peoples of the world do respond, not understanding those decisions but, in total unawareness of their frailty, supposing that the best has been decided upon. Otherwise (as even scholars have argued) why would advisors support or tolerate such decisions? The answer to that question has just been given in broad terms; more particularly, every head of state was nominated for office (and his election by popular vote or the vote of his immediate colleagues in a politburo was secured) through agreement within an existing elite that he could be directed and managed to the benefit of those who nominated him. All regimes are in this sense self-perpetuating. I cannot conceive how succession to office can be achieved otherwise, short of civil war and revolution. But once having

49

elected a leader, the elite who hoped to direct and manage him finds itself in much the same situation as the rest of the citizenry does; the leader's willingness to make decisions places an exaggerated and unintended power in his hands. Few can feasibly make much headway in opposing a ruler. When questioned and put on the defensive, decisive persons are made more than usually stubborn in defending their opinions, since they fear to reflect upon their choices. From the beginning it was their talent not to be overly aware of alternatives. If made aware, they then feel themselves swallowed up in a morass of conflicting good ends amidst which—being unpracticed at extricating themselves—they lose direction and cannot decide anything. To expose decisive people is to destroy them; to destroy them is to return again to immobility. It may thus not be compassion for a boss but everyone's self-interest that protects rulers from humiliation.

The dangers that I have just outlined are real enough, especially when the fate of humanity hangs upon them; therefore constitutional remedies have been developed. But the weakness of any national constitution is that it prescribes behavior applicable almost solely to high government officials: the head of state, legislators, high court judges and the like. In a constitutional crisis it is only these same officials who can legally decide whether their conduct is consistent with the spirit of the constitution from which they derive their authority to judge themselves. National referenda alter this conclusion no more than national elections do since any issue or candidate voted upon was already determined by these same officials. Conscience, good will, a keen sense of trusteeship in caring for the community: these alone guarantee responsible interpretations of a national constitution. It would be foolish to write off moral rectitude as an unlikely trait in political leaders despite the narrowness of their vision; it is more likely that this same narrowness accounts for their abiding by legal formalities, which

Leaders, Laws, And Justice

more imaginative men might well scorn. It is extraordinary that the general spirit of constitutional arrangements has been so closely and so consistently honored. If poets, thespians, speculators in commodities, and political philosophers were to occupy high political offices of unlimited discretion, a sense of humor and of high drama would certainly lead them to reorder playfully all inconvenient aspects of any constitution. They would realize that even the most glaring reordering of governmental procedures will hardly disturb anyone's sleep so long as the changes are clothed in pretentious dignity and proclaimed to be rediscoveries of the most solemn rights and privileges long the possession of a happy populace. Some part of this pantomime has accompanied every twist of constitutional evolution from the days of Chief Justice Coke to Chief Justice Warren.

Pantomime or not, the characteristic means for remedying human behavior arises out of the character of leadership which I have been describing. Decisive persons recognize events as being bounded, often without alternatives and with an imperative to act. Events are seen not as aspects of some system within other systems amid a universe of interdependent parts, but as causes preceding effects along a single linear track. Given this view of events, a leader is chiefly concerned to line up everyone's behavior according to this linear perspective: he tells those about him to march eastward and to pass the word until all are marching eastward. He is then himself constrained by his own instructions to go east, a victim of his own propaganda. He finds himself promulgating a general law and must live under its authority, as if he had given away his own powers of decision to some unseen Master of Events, force of history. Reflection upon this phenomenon must first have suggested the notion that gods and not men ruled events, and that their rule was arbitrary and unhinderable, as the Laws of Nature were and later certain inexplicable events (such as the force of gravity) are today.

51

Law is undoubtedly the most brilliant of human inventions because it brings to everyone a leader's voice and intention. A law can be carried by word of mouth from person to person throughout a large population with hardly any diminishment of its impact, because it is a simple command. It possesses no subtlety; it is as clear in its narrowness of vision, its lack of qualification, as the leader's vision which conceived it. Since animals likewise live by rules, law cannot have been an invention independent of any natural models from which to copy, though the same is true of nearly everything else: a rolling stone suggested the wheel. But human or positive law should never be confounded with laws of the natural sciences. The hallmark of social law is its arbitrariness, its command that behavior be ordered in given ways regardless of other circumstances, while laws of natural phenomena pretend to represent or describe operations that would have happened without human interference. (There has been great confusion on this point: most social scientific models mistake arbitrary, legalistic commands for presumed processes of natural social phenomena, and consequently the models are said to demonstrate the presence of inherent conditions when actually they demonstrate only that a particular behavior can be consummated upon command.) In short, law is an extension of leadership enculturated into habit. It is an institutionalization of particular leaders' commands and continues to direct people for as long as it is reinforced through childhood training and public deference.

The peculiar character of general laws is best understood by contrasting the two earliest forms of human expression before a public audience: stories, legends, and poetry on the one hand; laws, regulations, and commands on the other. Primitive storytelling is rich in allusion and suggestion; it is a holistic comprehension of interdependent subtleties, a sort of circular view of existence. Primitive law is usually codified into a series of absolute and unequivocal commands. It seems impossible that

52

the same mind could have conceived both, and I have already proposed that the peculiar character of laws issues from the peculiar limitations of political mentality. Thus, the best remedy for the arbitrariness of general laws would seem to be a compensating implementation of more holistic, poetic insights about the character of human events. Poets and philosophers might well be placed in a circle around every leader to broaden his perspective, modify his judgments, aid him to understand what he performs. Some part of this recommendation has always been utilized in every polity, but broadening a ruler's perspective works against the reason why he arose in the first place. Rulers neither seize leadership nor are elected or appointed in order to explicate the human situation; their task is to resolve it by choosing one or another arbitrary course of action. Poets are concerned with explaining acts of the gods or the mysteries of love or with reconciling us to the corruption of all things. But leaders act within a general view of those matters already encultured by poets, and therefore leaders lean upon poets for support (or if poets fail to support the regime, leaders in self-interest must censor them and demand more chauvinistic literature). In any case the remedy for constitutional measures that fail to curb leaders' powers could seldom if ever be a broadening of leaders' insights, lest they thereby lose their capacity for decision. Instead, leaders unconsciously curb themselves by law-making; they bind themselves by their own acts. Yet everyone else is no less bound, so that poets no longer sing just any song but must (in my example) celebrate an eastward march.

Aligning a whole population in this way gradually involves decisions of the ruler's lieutenants as the polity's services become more various (independent of its size). The polity comes to require more specialized decisions, which force the development of professions, perhaps dividing areas of decision between public and private spheres of activity. Rulers cannot now issue detailed instructions for everyone's behavior. They therefore employ a personal staff to speak in their place who, together with all other public and private executives, form a ruling elite, proportional in size to the tasks necessary for a given community's care. Such elites need guidance of the same sort that they in turn provide ordinary citizens. Such guidance takes the form of codified commands and regulations because that is how rulers tend to think; the psychological bias inherent in the leadership function thus infects the operation of every polity. Any society thus becomes dependent upon law, custom, and a given political culture, and will defend that culture as if deviations from it were a crime against the eternal and absolute right order of things. Respect for law does not arise from its having solved anyone's personal problem; law has assured only the minimal cooperation necessary for the community's care, not anyone's personal good, except indirectly as when he arranges his financial affairs to benefit from legal circumstance. In this sense law is amoral, if morality is the good of particular persons. It is moot whether any moral crusade in support of any humanly conceived system of commands is morally justified. However that be, crusades are unnecessary since any polity has a propensity to collapse inwardly in proportion as the manifest injustice of the applications of particular laws to particular situations or persons multiplies, and there ensues a deterioration of morale. All regimes are thus vulnerable to criticism and to constant change following such criticism. It is therefore deemed inherent wisdom that there be institutions for voicing criticism and facilitating change.

It should be comforting that at least the community which supports and bears us forward, like a ship upon the ocean, is extraordinarily seaworthy. But it can also be under the command of a tyrannical captain whose orders to the helmsman and regulations for the passengers' safety make no sense to us standing at the rail, judging the oncoming seas, and not altogether ignorant of seamanship. Talking together, telling each other how we feel, considering whether we should interfere or propose a new captain and what would happen in that event—these have the significant result of lightening our moods and making us feel better for having unburdened ourselves. It has always been so. A woman's tears, a man's anger, a child's boasting remake their self-knowledge into new self-experience. The function of meeting together is to share and present in some form observable by another the conceptual vortex that each takes to be reality, but which seems doubtful, maybe a dream or a nightmare, if not confirmed by someone else's recognition of its plausibility. Within ourselves impressions pass us by, one after another, as if almost anything could be somehow true or false, painful or exhilarating. We construct conceptions of reality like window glass, through which we observe these impressions, believing or disbelieving them as they correlate with our former conceptions of reality, our cumulative measure of the believable. Being aware of this self-deluding, self-preserving trickery, we need others to tell us that our impressions are justified, a fair estimate of what has happened and will happen. The substance of justice among us is no more than reassurance by one another that our realities are justified—not that our realities are identical, which is impossible, each of us knowing his own world in his own way, but plausible and understandable to others so that we can live together, not alone. Were justice some single truth independent of personal need, it might be interesting to God but unknowable also. Justice is either a touchstone upon which everyone can lay his hand or else belongs to none of us and is only an idle curiosity.

If people are not open to one another's hurts no justice can be done. And if they lie to one another there can be no foundation of mutual confidence to support each other's further needs. If they misconstrue how well each understands the other and what burdens they can carry for one another, so that together they live upon false expectations, the community becomes unjust to each in proportion as each has failed to perceive the others' claims. A just community depends upon openness, integrity, and knowledge of itself. A community is not whole without being just. Care for its wholeness is the responsibility of rulers, although commanding people to be open toward one another, to exercise integrity, and to understand what they can do for each other only partially fulfills that responsibility. Setting an example is certainly the greater part of the leader's task. Lack of example in international relationships directly discourages integrity in national governments and also extends corruption into the future, as children mimic the great men in their elders' generation.

There must be occasions for exchanges of reassurance between rulers and ruled whereby the warp and woof of just relationships is woven ever more securely. For this reason councils (in which to counsel one another) and meetings (in which to meet one another, commune, agree) multiply in a just society. Their scarcity impedes development of any community. It is entirely possible that a meeting of minds through councils of rulers and some of the ruled (who then exchange that meeting of minds with others until a just rather than expedient consensus can result) might bring about the same reassurance achievable among close friends. The great barrier to it is the single-eyed righteousness of leaders and bosses already described. Nor have I any expectation of some new form of leadership, of philosopher kings. Is there thus any reasonable hope for a just society? I do not know. The worst mistake is to foreclose possibilities. I can conceive of gradual understanding simultaneously embracing people's need for justice and an awareness of the social situation generally (our interdependence, care of the community, relationships of rulers and ruled, limits of political activity). While the character of leadership does not change as a result, yet people's positive responses to that leadership would require leaders to be more just. But all this is merely hopeful.

A sort of justice arises in sportsmanship. By their acts in the midst of intense competition, players can reassure each other that they share the same reality enveloping them all, that together they both win and lose regardless of the score. The test of strength, endurance, and skill must not humble the losers nor intoxicate the winners. Equally the spectators must identify themselves with the logic of fruitful rather than destructive competition, or injustice will certainly be done. The game can become an occasion for political education as can a stage play or other spectacle insulated against the humdrum of ordinary living. Spectators and players can share the need that everything come out all right in the end, as in a children's fairy tale where, because the magic prince is ultimately wise and good, the losers are succored, and the winners win only for the sake of showing how well the losers lost.

Justice is done whenever, in place of righteousness untempered by care of others, there arises an understanding that men are not owed anything beyond what each can do for the other which, because they are interdependent, benefits the giver as well as the receiver. Were people equal in any sense, equal treatment of everyone would constitute justice for all. But since such equality is obviously untrue, and since an equal distribution of anything or of all things would be disproportionate to people's needs, there will always be the strong and the weak. The strong must aid the weak and the weak depend upon the strong without any possibility of equal exchange or of compensation to the strong for their sacrifices. A society in which the help of the strong is enlisted through promises of abundant reward is corrupted because then the weak must support not only themselves but also the strong, making the strong ever stronger, the weak ever weaker. Insofar as the strong misunderstand this justice or never glimpse it at all, often supposing justice to be something blind and abstract, the whole meaning of human interdependence—and therefore of social organization and human survival—is fatally obscured. Such misunderstanding has resulted in holding back the greater part of humanity's potentialities and in fantastic miseries, degradation, and exploitation. The schoolboy's view of history is that of a chronicle of continuous crime amorally celebrated.

It would be foolish to suppose that any truly just regimes have ever existed or else Christ and the saints would not have preached but merely pointed to examples of what rulers and ruled had already accomplished. Yet it would be equally short-sighted to suppose that we are all not waiting for justice, and that we do not expect its coming. This expectation finally permits leaders to rule, and is disregarded at peril to the whole human venture.

VI.

THE MANAGEMENT OF POLITIES

Any law is reducible to a standard of performance. Actual performance measured against that standard is subject to ever-changing circumstance—the weather, people's health, their training and talents. The problem of law-making then becomes not merely what kinds of activity to command or how such commands should be administered but the level of performance to which laws may prompt people to aspire. If that level is so low as to absorb almost all contingencies, the material culture can never be very rich. It is true that poverty may prevent the majority from indulging in "cheap extravagance," as it appears to cultivated eyes, and often makes feasible the employment of specialized artisans on a few triumphs of artistry and taste. Low performance permits leisure for both rich and poor since their time is not absorbed by continuous schooling or by the use and care of machinery and instrumentation; there is no problem of filling a vast and continual demand for minerals, agricultural produce, transportation, and communication.

But primitive economy does not yield a more open society than modern industrialization does. The relatively restricted rounds of repetitive work in primitive economies leave fewer occasions for distraction from boredom, and aggravate frustration at others' stubbornness and idiosyncrasies. Exact records and nice calculations are impossible in a primitive economy; people easily cheat each other by hiding part of a crop contrary to customs of pooling village resources. Secret arrangements abound and corrupt the polity. Consequences can be direct and terrible for those concerned although the processes of material production are in no way altered—the quantity and quality of new crops are at the mercy of weather and previous agronomic ignorance regardless of the fate of the former crop. But in a technologically oriented society, falsification of records or on-the-job behavior, kept secret from others, will cause further miscalculations that, multiplied throughout an interdependent economy embracing millions of persons, inhibit or destroy the capacity to produce a good living for anyone. Not all great economic depressions or waste of resources in aimless wars have been caused by purposeful misinformation. But the daily costs of errors and misjudgments are so apparent to managers of sophisticated enterprises that none questions the absolute necessity for constant and full disclosure of every sort of information. Wherever there remains from a more primitive past the inclination to maintain the privacy of records, of behavior, even of thoughts, the whole complex of modern social existence is made proportionally unmanageable. Open disclosure may embarrass one's ego; yet it becomes not merely interpersonally virtuous but essential to the integration of interdependent social, industrial, and governmental activities everywhere across the globe. A more just polity (in my meaning of justice) is achieved through the operation of this paradox. As people in a technologically advanced culture are required to lead more disciplined and demanding lives with less opportunity to indulge their own or others' whims or to tolerate idiosyncrasies, they are also required to be more open, generous, and understanding in order to comprehend one another's activities. Unless they know what others have already done and will likely do, they cannot foresee and prepare their future roles.

I assume that a more just society is desirable and that the simple life has been left behind. All the foregoing implies that standards of performance must be high rather than low. But standards set too high discourage the less able and deplete their morale. When this happens, when the very most that someone can contribute is too little, the society is left short-handed. The task, then, is to stimulate achievement. For this, fixed standards, rules commanding a given output of energy or insight, are peculiarly inappropriate since they demand too little from some, too much from others. The laws of a primitive community constitute bounds beyond which people are forbidden to trespass. Mere necessity and want are believed sufficient to stimulate whatever slight technological and intellectual capacity that people may possess. Law tends to be a series of negative commands telling people what not to do, requiring little judgment beyond determining the facts of trespass. The circumstances of abundant and rapidly evolving technology require not laws forbidding disobedience or fixed standards setting minimum outputs of energy, but undefined standards of high expectation competitively achieved. An undefined but high expectation sets no bounds of necessity or want, and it cannot be enforced by citing trespass or easily demonstrable negligence. Rather, competition must determine the standard; there are no limits of achievement, no ceilings on performance.

These undefined standards of expectation, applied to a whole population's social, economic, and political behavior, place everyone in a game with everyone else. The entire character of the culture is radically altered from that of more primitive societies. There appear to be no boundaries separating permissible from impermissible behavior. High achievement so often overleaps old prejudice, or so often involves possibilities never before envisaged, that it appears to the players not a game involving others within agreed rules for some definite prize; nor a game with impartial umpires by which some win and others lose; but at best a game of solitaire where scientists, administrators, and professional persons (and even, by imitation, unskilled workers) work each in his own way to achieve self-imposed goals. Yet one's work in turn establishes demands for materials that others must supply. A whole train of consequences is set in motion. Everyone must consume what is offered to him by everyone else or, rejecting it, has nothing to use in developing his own product. He must continually adapt his way of life to new material conditions. A little of the same can be said of any society at any level of material and intellectual interdependence, but in a primitive economy mutual accommodation takes place over many lifetimes while it is required throughout every year in an advanced one.

Such great accommodation suggests the possibility of a self-regulative polity in which, having schooled everyone to accept an undefined standard of high achievement, every citizen would boss himself; he would decide what he must do and how he should cooperate with everyone else. Such was the model of a laissez faire market economy (though based upon assumptions borrowed from village economies, where necessity rather than enculturation supposedly dictated exchange at personal profit). It was also the model of international relationships where countervailing ambitions of national statesmen supposedly led to successive accommodations of diplomatic influence and military force. The logic of both models required complete information of everyone's intentions and actions; and so likewise does the logic of utilizing high personal achievement standards in an interdependent polity. This logic has been realized in actual practice beyond any reasonable expectation of former generations. Yet everyone still lives in a world of deficient persons—the very young, the senile, the stupid, the sick, the brilliant—so that for all our efforts there is neither enough information nor a sufficient number of able persons for us to achieve any semblance of a self-regulative polity. Instead, all these interpersonal accommodations must be guided, stimulated, or retarded as everyone's benefit may dictate. The inherently competitive character of interacting (though individually monitored) standards of high achievement must be umpired, not by calling foul but by foreseeing the consequences of one player's behavior upon others. Such foresight is no more than the social and economic planning with which we are already familiar, and such political planning as we must now prepare to accept.

From the point of view of all who regulate the consequences of others' achievements, it is the greatest good fortune that the potentials of human achievement are barely understood and no doubt vastly under-utilized. Greater knowledge entails greater effort; for every increase in the quantity and kind of endeavor —dependent upon and engendering other quantities and kinds —the whole complex of people's relationships must be adjusted. Existing outlets for expression burst apart. Frustration must be channelled away. Ever more persons are employed to alleviate others' disappointment or hurt pride, or even to answer their questions. New achievements bring new costs of obsolescence, depletion, and waste. Such costs stimulate innovation or call down legislation to restrain their development. I speak as if regulators of a society could anticipate these consequences of others' achievement but, even were that true, much knowledge could not be used effectively. Knowledge of others' blindness is still filtered through minds themselves deficiently insightful, less than wise. Orders are not fully grasped or obeyed. Especially is this true of fiscal management. People misinterpret their part in the whole, over-react, or cannot fit their interests to the demands of those trying to regulate the total economic system. These sorts of fallibility open opportunity for others to try to fulfill those demands and thus find personal advantage. It is the great virtue of developed societies that one man's failure induces another to supply what the first failed to supply; thus a constant flow of goods and services is provided. Yet at the same time it is then profitable for some to misinform their fellows or otherwise induce their failure, for which everyone collectively must pay even while a few gain relatively to the rest. From this point forward a general corruption of the polity is extremely easy, easier than corruption of a village economy and government.

A society of competitive achievers is complexly articulated. A few rulers continue to rule in the old way, issuing commands; a far larger number is deputized to regulate and manage the effects of citizen activity just described; a still larger body pursues new achievements of every sort; and then there are all those who teach techniques of achievement and of adjustment to them; and finally there are the students, apprentices, and assistants in these pursuits who are too young or too old or otherwise unfit, and must await their turn to participate or merely to benefit. Opportunity increases for people to take advantage of others' labor, to pretend achievement where none exists, to seek the favor of managers of the polity.

Such corruption of the purposes and design of a society is not new in kind but only in extent. The society is now so rich in diversity of occupations, in specialized techniques for their conduct, and in overlap and interdependence that its design and consequently its management is impossible for any single mind to appreciate except in principle rather than in concrete detail. More primitive social systems are manageable because they merely rely upon each person's self-interest in doing what lies before him—though by methods that hardly advance his interest, and that leave him physically deprived and emotionally frustrated—but his fate is his alone and hurts few others, probably only his family. In primitive social systems, isolated families rot, each on its own stalk like wildflowers in a meadow; in our present culture, millions are intertwined like a gigantic vine reaching up to cover the ruins of all previous cultures, although the single root of the vine is exposed, and anyone strong enough to hack it through can destroy the whole. The vital sap of this vine is competitive performance; some who have succeeded competitively and have strength to cut the root may always suppose that cutting it would make them master of all, or at least put everyone else under mortal obligation to them. The notion of monopoly of goods, services, or military force gains significance from these reflections. Within a national economy or within the world polity of nation states, schemes of monopoly have had continuous appeal. Trade unions monopolize particular services to protect their members from monopolies of employers or consumers, and vice versa. Groups within a monopoly seek control of the monopoly's monopoly. The same consideration explains the behavior of political factions within an urban or national polity.

I seem to have confounded two separate matters: corruption of the political system through seeking special favor or taking advantage of others' labor, and the consequences of unregulated competition. But they are actually the same. They consist in excluding others from some benefit that might have come to them. I have argued that exclusion is politically dysfunctional and am confirmed in this opinion by the early history of competitive capitalism and by the history of international competition.

The case is further complicated by the anomaly that rulers tend to think, and consequently to act, in terms of fixed standards of performance but are disinclined to be bounded by such standards when competing with one another. They command but are not easily commanded, until feedback from their own commands limits their future options of behavior. The result of this anomaly is that leaders of highly regulated societies fail to submit to regulations by one another, and by their example unconsciously corrupt the very systems that they strive to maintain. A leader's self-confidence is his most essential attribute and cannot be damaged without destroying his usefulness. His single-eyed vision drives him forward to win the game (since what else are games for, he asks?) without considering the total situation within which games are played and which constitutes a supportive environment. That total situation is everyone's interdependence. Since interdependence reaches as far as the affairs of any person may affect the affairs of any others (today, the world's population), damage to any must affect all the rest in varying degree.

This oldest and most obvious of all political problems must be solved in every political culture or the culture collapses; corruption of this sort is no more inherent than disease germs in an animate body but is equally endemic and requires some spontaneous response. At this moment that response is the activity of professional persons all over the world whose undefined standards of competitive achievement cause them to cooperate in maintaining public health, controlling trade, exchanging information—while contradictorily world political leaders impede or forbid these very activities in order to gain immediate advantage from games of monopolizing influence or status. Neither of these opposing actions is historically unusual; the same sort of conflict between leaders and their chief servants, this working at cross purposes, is always to be expected. Nothing else can be anticipated from the future.

Do professional persons, including civil servants who cooperate to maintain the present world polity, have the good of everyone in mind and do they always take the right measures, while world political leaders out of stubborn self-interest always take the wrong? Probably the most important difference between the two is their situation: the leader stands exposed in the front rank, all eyes upon him, having to speak out and initiate seemingly without hesitation, while the others watch in the shadows behind the leader, judging his stance and its effects relative to his intentions and to events. Though I have dramatized and no doubt exaggerated the character of leadership talents, yet obviously there is no sharp division between those possessing these talents and those lacking them. Many in the shadows may be as righteously single-eyed as a leader standing in the limelight but they are not compelled by all those particular circumstances which brought the leader to accept his position. Their critical and evaluative talents are thereby liberated and evoked while the leader's are distracted and suppressed by self-consciousness of his role. These relationships are not different from those of a father speaking out in a family dispute who cannot judge his own actions as well as those around him can; he is guided better by his wife or son or daughter, who is concerned not only for him but for the welfare of all involved, than by his own will, or by the whole neighborhood which lacks intimate knowledge of him. High civil servants, like leaders, are compelled by their position within the polity as much as by the talents which may have brought them to those positions; neither civil servant nor leader may be wise but each finds himself in a given position, one to judge, the other to act. A great part of what traditionally was deemed the judicial function in fact falls upon civil administrators, in cases of conflict involving their political masters as well as ordinary citizens.

The care of the community is not thereby lifted from leaders' shoulders but increasingly is implemented by permanent officials long familiar with the convolutions of customary conduct. It is also true that such convolutions frustrate direct action; therefore leaders less concerned with accustomed procedures more readily accomplish the impossible. Yet as already mentioned, leaders unconsciously corrupt the very systems that they strive to maintain, for which the only remedy is regulation of political games by those close enough to understand those games. Whether corruption occurs by stealth despite political procedures outlawing it or openly for lack of such procedures, civil servants are in the best position to discover it and judge its extent and practical cure. Therefore they regulate almost every activity of modern nations, performing a vast and intricate operation affecting everyone's behavior throughout the world. Though, as previously described, princes must monitor themselves, yet just as princes can rule only insofar as their followers respond positively, so can they rule only insofar as their chief servants carry out their wishes. It is thus entirely possible (and for great stretches of history has been true) that chief servants, mayors of the palace, in fact preserve the polity while their masters contribute the ability to decide matters when wiser or more sensitive men would hesitate. It then becomes the task of chief servants to turn these decisions into fruitful channels: to avoid wars when otherwise their masters would precipitate them, to maintain public health despite disputes over who shall take the credit for it, to facilitate trade among enemies, to exchange information even when leaders cannot imagine how any view contrary to their own could be significant. I conclude that responsibility for preventing corruption and for maintaining conditions where justice is possible must devolve upon the officers of bureaucracies.

If this responsibility can be maintained proportionally to world-wide awareness of world community, higher civil servants must necessarily cooperate across national boundaries and jurisdictions. Leading civil servants of the world must gradually form a single profession in constant interaction and communication. Its object would be to keep the peace of the globe.

Competition or confrontation cannot take place except through preparation of the grounds for it. In simple polities, leaders prepare their own confrontations by arguing within their own minds the possible advantages and disadvantages, the strength of their ambition and extent of their energy. In modern polities leaders are helpless without professional assessment of everything necessary to bring about a given result; a military campaign no longer consists in the charge of a Light Brigade and so demands decades of preparation. The vast majority of persons involved, like foot soldiers, may have small idea of what is transpiring; coordination and marshalling of events must lie with those who know better than anyone else what is going on and its limitations. These people cannot be leaders of the sort I have described. They must have technical competence, which relies upon openness to error, consideration of alternative assumptions, minds accustomed to believing that every prediction is a mere hypothesis. These are therefore not leaders but planners, not executives but staff officers.

Planners and staff officers do not regulate competition but merely supply the means for it. Between those preparing the means and leaders determining the ends stand chief civil servants and, in many nations, amateur public officials appointed to prepare for war or extend national interests or otherwise arrange tomorrow's events. But whether the means are adequate is a matter of judgment, in turn derived from the hypotheses of technically minded personnel. Hypotheses can as easily justify implementing political demands as they can disregarding those demands. The fulcrum of rational persuasion lies exactly here. And yet heads of state need not be swayed. They suspect from long experience that almost anything can be made to seem what it is not. Nevertheless their brittle self-confidence, their fear of being unhorsed by having to reconsider alternatives which their capacity for leadership long ago shunted aside in favor of righteous decision, can be jolted without destroying that self-confidence. Every advisor of princes knows this art. The apparent weight of technical assessments interpreted by chief civil servants can be brought to modify, retard, and even turn the course of leaders' action.

Such curbing of leaders remains haphazard if it is unorganized and has no leadership of its own, and therefore leaves every chief civil servant wondering what else he can do except advance a politician's demands. Leadership of civil servants among themselves could not be political but professional; otherwise civil servants would have to act the part of princes for which they are not suited and, logically, they would oust their masters. Professional leadership by colleagues of one another is perhaps not leadership at all but conscience—the reverse of righteous decision, a mere concern for appropriateness within broad limits, for general objectives with sufferance of deviations, for the integrity of causes without personal interest in dominating or profiting from them. These talents and perspectives are foreign to politics, have been drawn into serving modern governments only due to those changes of political culture described earlier in this chapter. The proof of their peculiar character is that whenever, through professional societies, attempts have been made to mobilize these talents and perspectives for particular political causes, the result has been to alienate and fragment the membership. Therefore, political leaders who might try to seize leadership of the civil services of one or several nations would only destroy those services. A professional responsibility among high civil servants of all nations for keeping world peace would only come about through mutual understanding without a formal leadership or a formal government superseding those governments employing them. In large part such an understanding has already grown between professionals in many disciplines and has been the chief means of forming present world culture.

I envisage gradual growth of an international profession of governmental practice by ways familiar in the development of all other professions. There must first be the occasion for it as I have already outlined. Yet that opportunity must be realized by the idea of a profession, implying an eventual body of knowledge sufficient to support generalization and application. In this sense there has never been a single profession of the arts but only schools of artistic endeavor; a profession requires some broad but specific goal, concretely achievable. The profession of civil service possessed such a goal at least a century ago. It needs now only a broadening of its horizon, a moving forward of its aims and a willingness to assume responsibility for them.

VII.

THE NEXT REVOLUTION

I can conceive of civil servants establishing a profession in which there would be a manageable conflict of loyalties between themselves and the world's rulers. Neither can dispense with the other. Rulers must generally accept what their civil services offer them while civil servants know very well the necessity for maintaining rulers in office. Dedication to world peace by chief civil servants would deprive the world's leadership of the means to threaten and coerce one another.

The higher civil services of every nation would form a worldwide profession by realizing their common interest and need to share their expertise. At first such an association would undoubtedly be interested primarily in technical questions of conducting their daily work: how best to recruit, train, and compensate employees; the collection and use of information; the care and feeding of elected officials; the development and implementation of programs; the reconciliation of divergent concepts and aims of differing legal systems throughout the globe; the rates at which separate or conflicting ways of managing national economies and judicial and cultural establishments might converge to reduce the inconveniences of international intercourse. The start of an international profession of civil servants would undoubtedly involve discussion of matters already explored in academic studies, as indeed now takes place insofar as civil servants participate in professional associations.

Inevitably the academic approach is more concerned for description and technique than for ends sought. This has been so both because political direction from the beginning of social organization has lain with political leaders rather than with observers of it, and because for the same reason social studies are assumed to have no normative influence upon policy-making. Although scholars rightly consider themselves the worst of possible leaders and although they seek purely to analyze events as if their own conclusions would not affect those events, yet any study of relationships immediately suggests potentially different relationships; any study thus becomes an instrument for normative development either by reinforcing existing norms through supposing that they constitute the experience of history, or by exposing their illogic. The same would be true of prolonged reflection among civil servants brought together from various nations. But unlike scholars they could never imagine themselves uninvolved in practical affairs. Just as boards and councils of policy-planners have been unable to free their deliberations from immediate political crises, so civil servants discussing their craft would find it difficult to ignore particular negotiations currently underway; they would have to take great pains to avoid recruiting one another into this or that cause; they would have to understand how far to count upon each other's political education rather than political action; they would have to judge the consequences of any restraining of their masters' ambitions.

I can conceive of present universities inviting members of international commissions and inter-govermental agencies to discuss their problems with each other and with scholars. The purpose would not be to inform university members of the great world outside, but to increase these diplomatic and quasi-diplomatic persons' understanding of each other's situations in their own governments. Much of this already happens although it is generally directed to justifying particular acts by government leaders rather than to exploring the more crucial question of what causes public servants to think as they do, what images of one another across international boundaries impel them to act as they have. The effect of such interchange may not be great; it may be clumsy and defensive. High civil servants are not apt to have the capacity for personal confession or the interest in exposing themselves to others' inquiry without obvious benefit for themselves or their masters. Nevertheless a start could be made by establishing a limited number of international schools for bringing together civil servants from all nations who would teach one another their life experiences, come to know and trust one another, and leave scholars increasing knowledge of what needs to be done to integrate the bureaucracies of all nations.

Such a scheme does not have the difficulty of another which I mentioned formerly. If all the world's leaders had once been school fellows in one or another international university and thus could know one another's backgrounds, temperaments, and sources of knowledge, then a vast amount of international tension would at once be removed. If one head of state were known by the rest to be incapable of telling the truth even to his closest friends, all others would understand how to deal with him. It is doubtful that he could even have come to office since his nomination would have triggered counter-moves by others of greater integrity; a self-protective elite of world leadership would inevitably result. But, unless leaders be chosen from an established aristocracy, their common education is impossible. Moreover it is obvious that leaders cannot be trusted to aid one another or grasp the universal elements of viable political existence, else they would long ago have exhibited these capacities. The best that can be anticipated is that leaders be prevented from destroying one another through guidance from those civil servants upon whom they must rely to implement that destruction.

Is it unlikely or impossible that political leaders would permit their civil service staffs to associate, for fear of just such brakes upon their own behavior? The short answer is that such restriction on association would expose the game now perpetrated upon mankind. The longer answer is that to the degree that leaders forbid interchange among their servants, spy upon them, distrust them, warn them against exposing the national interest to abuse, each leader is deprived of the quality of information and morale among his servants which is needed to checkmate or destroy another leader. Failure to permit interchange among civil services can only weaken any government; but there then is opportunity for some governments to become collectively more effective than the remainder by consolidating the mutual expertise of their combined civil services. Such an event could persuade the rest to follow their example. Development toward an international polity might thus be initiated.

The still longer answer is that it might be possible some day to do without leadership of the traditional sort at the world or even the national level. It is difficult to conceive that management of a world polity will differ in kind from management of lesser polities. And yet it has been only half a century since the means for very large scale central direction of nearly every human activity has been available. Over this short time it is increasingly evident that, though political bosses of the traditional sort are still essential for mobilizing opinion, saying come and go, these bosses often fail to enlist the sympathies of the professional staffs upon whom they must rely or to comprehend the information and make the careful judgments by which vast managerial complexes exist. There has been so far no new, alternative political style and no sign of its coming. But it can be imagined that gradually two distinct layers of political command may be necessary. It could be the function of one tier of command to arouse activity, to create and direct the self-awareness of local or even national communities; a separate tier could manage all those requisites of any community that only the very informed need ever know about, since they are beyond judgment by anyone else and involve no fundamental dispute. Management of a world currency and fiscal system, of world food supplies, of protection from pollution, of public health and medical care, of education, of communication, transportation, and power resources: these are examples of matters which require not leadership of the old sort, but "non-political" leadership. Such a fanciful picture raises many questions. This second and non-political layer of world leadership above national and local leaders could arise informally among officials of international agencies dealing with just such matters as international trade, world food supplies, and the other concerns mentioned. The whole development might go unnoticed until it had already become established. And such a leadership might find itself able then to insist that civil servants of every nation be permitted to associate with them, while still maintaining the present means for conducting national affairs.

However it may in the end be accomplished, it is safe to assume that professional persons of all nations will ever more continuously exchange ideas and techniques despite national rivalries. Among these are already many high civil servants. The process must advance. It is then necessary to elicit tolerance if not positive response from the world's citizenry—long enculturated as it is to suspect subversion of local custom and moralities by individuals talking a different language of concepts and more tolerant of variety than ordinary men. It is therefore obvious that great attention must be paid to how any international community of civil servants and others is reported in mass media. Writers should be employed to set the tone of reporting, to make it understandable and yet undramatic, so that it does not become a political event. Any less care could only further retard world community. The whole difficulty of speaking quietly about anything concerned with public interest appears insurmountable. Secrecy is almost always an evil, and shouting hardly less so. Yet consensus is a fact of political existence, as already noted, and is necessary for polities to exist at all. Consensus is obtained by a million small voicings of opinion, by willingness to think well of what already appears to have been accepted.

If tolerance of concern for world peace is obtainable, then perhaps general laws setting boundaries to the behavior of national and sub-national governments are also. Laws limiting personal or institutional behavior are equally unenforceable except if persons or officials have achieved a prior consensus to obey them. It thus could happen that in proportion as the world's civil services became prepared to honor one another's commitments to preserve the peace of the globe, political leaders might tolerate laws governing their own behavior rather than submit to informal guidance through civil servants. Leaders could then explain their peaceableness better as obedience to law than as inability to circumvent the conciliatory efforts of their own government servants.

I seem to speak as if all political problems were merely those of governments, rather than also of peoples encultured to hate one another, and in many cases excluded from participation with other citizens of their "own" nations. I do not mean to forget how far from any politically viable existence so many of the earth's people have been driven by traditions and deficiencies, independently of governmental action. While the political function is the care of the whole human community, governments can only set up conditions for people's inclusion among one another, not guarantee the result. Establishment of these conditions could be made the responsibility of national leaders everywhere, if they were developed and made administrably feasible by a world civil service. Similarly might the use of any military forces be brought within the range of all leaders' collective responsibility. I suspect that these developments may be more easily understood than measures for preserving and enhancing our natural environment, or for providing minimal services to all the world's population, because these last could require regulation of the size of population and perhaps its geographical distribution.

The product of such day-dreaming may be merely the conclusion that while more primitive polities require leaders to bring them into existence, the more sophisticated world polity needs additional leadership of a new kind. This leadership cannot at the present moment expect to elicit consensus simultaneously from all the world's population; that population is too diverse. But such a leadership could arise upon the shoulders of traditional leadership concerned with resolving the indecisiveness of ordinary citizens. The new leadership could act not as a catalyst of popular opinion but as advisors of princes; their task would be the care of princes as the task of princes is the care of national and local communities. What I suggest is a means for regulating competition among "sovereign" governments and their heads of state. That the suggestion may seem extraordinary is partly explained away by remembering that in the history of capitalism, regulation of captains of industry was more self-initiated than imposed. As private capitalist empires grew in size and influence, their managements sought protection from destructive competition and even became concerned for the public benefit. They therefore suggested codes of fair business practice and proposed regulatory commissions to oversee and sanction their growth. That many of these commissions were incompetent suggests that failures of an internationally cohesive civil service need not doom a world community; it might similarly come about that national leaders would seek to strengthen the guidance that a world civil service could provide them. One can imagine world community without a chief executive, an association of nation states directed by general laws and by mutual counsel among leadership of various sorts collectively responsible for that community.

One consequence of the taming of international relationships may be to alter governmental policies from the heedless and headless sanction of unlimited expansion of every human enterprise, toward more conscientious examination of how far any enterprise may be pursued without threatening human survival. Another consequence might be to reveal those projects which cannot be delayed and to emphasize the necessity of their development. These matters are self-evident. They imply claims upon the intelligent and talented for their fellows' benefit, a respect for purposive behavior rather than appetite, and the need to reconcile people with whatever is essential for their opportunity to exist together.

But despite all the bright words that may ever be written, no one can promise any greater happiness in this more inclusive, open, and probably just world than heretofore. It is not for the sake of happiness that any of this should be done. It is merely necessary in the same way that leadership and other universal conditions of politics have proved necessary. Yet necessity in social affairs is an uncertain quantum because people generally act according to what they believe they should do rather than according to any necessity in events themselves. And even then, an act believed necessary may still not seem enough so to compel anyone's response.

POSTSCRIPT: PURELY ACADEMIC

I cannot resist the temptation to say a number of things which would have complicated and confused the book just written but which interest me as a teacher.

For instance, the matter of my cosmology. What is the most fundamental of all matters political? It is obviously the care of the human community. Very well, but is care of the community a Platonic idea inherent in some nature of things whether or not anyone realizes it? Oh no, not at all. Then, since I reject that answer, is care of the community a natural law in the sense used by Aquinas, i.e., deducible by rational men although events may well include a great deal else not deducible, since events embrace more than men can understand? Well, that meaning of care of the community comes closer to my thought, even though I do not worry about the totality of all things, which seems to me a bit irrelevant. Care of the human community is required by our particular situations of interdependence; we discover it not rationally through deduction from any first principles but intuitively from what we finally perceive as necessary when reconciled to our interdependence. It is possible to care for one another spontaneously in consequence of our merely being together and alive, a fact of our situation, rational or not, inherent or not. But obviously many are not reconciled to their interdependence, and do not care for one another. Am I saying, then, that they should be reconciled, that they should be brought in some way to care? And is the hidden thesis of this book a normative command to care, or the devil take us all?

Yes, for myself, care of others is the beginning of any wisdom about social intercourse. But my facts and conclusions need not be others'. Since I take facts to be what we believe we perceive, there is no secure reference from which my facts— and normative judgments flowing therefrom—can be proved fallible. Someone else can only believe them fallible on the authority of his own convictions. Difference of opinion and fallibility become the same thing. Is all scholarship and thought reduced merely to this, a conflict of arbitrary opinions? Much of it is not; for example, an historian accurately reports the contents of an archive, but takes no responsibility for the opinions in his sources, perhaps merely noting their disagreement. Yet in not supposing that one witness knew better than the other, he risks nothing and does not add knowledge or contribute to debate. Could I retreat to reliance upon culture patterns, claiming that care of one another is embedded within our folkways and should be recognized as the most fundamental of matters political? No, my view is really that despite culture, and despite others' disagreements with my model, I defy anyone to find a more successful way for conducting social existence than care of the human community. This is my limitation, my ground, where I begin. I could claim that all thought starts with *a priori* assumptions, but that statement does not distinguish between better and worse assumptions, and is a mere observation concerning epistemology. I prefer to rely for defense upon my defiance of others' better somewhere and arbitrarily chose my ground. Defiance opens somewhere and arbitrarily chose my ground. Defiance opens the way toward others' counter proposals. That suits my profession of teacher.

I am aware that Aquinas suggested to me the care of the community. But behind his conclusion lay the enormous structure of his thought, in turn induced from Christ's parables. Am I not, then, a mere creature of Christian culture? Why not admit it? I do, and yet the truth insofar as I know it is that I have looked upon Christ's parables and upon all else that I have studied or observed merely as human experience opened to our use, and useful to the extent that any of us try it out on our friends and families; they represent our social laboratory. Their behavior along with our own can never constitute a controlled experiment; better than that, it is a living experiment of mutual involvement. In our caring for one another (and in no other way) we discover whatever there is to be found, any science involved in our relationships, any justice, any polity actually existent. I cannot, therefore, recommend that students seek some abstract method or any natural laws or a profile of our culture as the means to understanding politics. Politics is amidst us or nowhere. Thus my challenge to others to invent a better ground for matters political is not that they search for some point in spacetime immune from human involvement, where all otherwise conflicting observations fall into a simple mechanical pattern; but that they stay right here amidst this living experiment. Trying to understand their involvement will better reveal whatever is necessary for explaining it than will trying to construct a "reality" never experienced.

Does all the rest of my model necessarily follow from the premise of our interdependence or from my solution that we should care for the community? No; there is slight necessity in the human affairs that I describe. But the rest of my model is at least intended to follow a logic of what is desirable. It is politically desirable to hold this human mess together, to rule. That seems self-evident. It was argued at considerable length. I am not satisfied that my recommendations would necessarily bring about what I claim; that result hinges on whatever is required to motivate people and on their non-political goals. All of which brings me to another difficulty.

There is no generally accepted model of human psychology that I could have used here. Existing models have no bio-

81

chemical foundation, and are wholly speculative. One seemingly specific psychology of individual behavior tells us that every response must have some stimulus; but it does not answer how any stimulus causes any behavior, or which stimuli account for which responses. An alternative supposition is that various traits or talents must permit some persons, but not others, to respond to given stimuli. Trait psychology does not answer why we possess these presumed traits, the extent to which they are utilized, or how their interaction produces a pattern of social behavior. My own supposition that only a few persons readily make decisions to which others must positively respond in order to form a polity is a similar social-psychological explanation and is also speculative.

Likewise I seem to have no sociology beyond a general hypothesis that social organization by leaders of responsive followers is a sociological datum explaining government. My difference with many modern writers is their temptation to push matters further. They believe that given social or economic conditions force given options for behavior upon people, and preclude other options—thus determining how people act toward one another, and determining in turn the institutional forms through which they act. Such writers claim that a set of comprehensive environmental stimuli affecting a whole population results in generalized reactions that require only a very general trend of historical events to confirm it. In Marx's terms, certain "material conditions" determine our awareness, virtually our thoughts, and provide readily observable data for a science of society. If one identifies a pattern of historical evolution and explains it by supposing a generalized response to initial general conditions, one arrives at Marx's science. It is a science because the fact of such an historical evolution confirms any hypothesis predicting just that evolution, and no alternative one. The sociology of knowledge is proved beyond doubt.

My first difficulty with Marx's model is the reliability of historical knowledge. Every generation reinterprets past records to suit contemporary prejudice, so that a secondary-source-history inevitably discovers an evolutionary development of which its participants were unaware. What participants did perceive (in the records left by them) were other patterns suited to their time. Each era lives within the walls of its own vision; each is a culture complete in itself. We cannot conclude that successive environmental stimuli caused one another but merely that certain phenomena have been ubiquitous, like the presence of leaders and led. I have tried to escape these difficulties. On the one hand I acknowledge the presence of cultures by avoiding any assumption that would turn out, with the hindsight of a future generation, to have been culture-bound; on the other hand I avoid any typology of cultures that would tempt me into a sociology (a culturally-causative explanation) of knowledge. Fastidiousness likewise forecloses postulating a science of politics. Until the bio-chemistry of human thought is revealed, or until the barrier of historicism is overcome, any science of social behavior must rest upon a positive correlation of given stimuli with given responses by the greater part of a whole population interacting together. That day has not arrived.

Meanwhile in my model the actions of leaders and any responses by the led are assumed to be culture-bound, without specifying either culture-content or the range of actions or of responses. My model therefore encompasses any actual evolution of behavior that might fit the sociology-of-knowledge hypothesis yet does not endorse that theory.

At a different level of explanation, it may be noticed that I leave aside economic justice and hardly mention economic organization. One of the biggest events of recent years has been the realization that our technology now allows an end to poverty; we could produce an adequate standard of living for everyone on earth. Two barriers stand in the way. One is political:

care of the community is not yet recognized as the overriding political consideration, and thus our technology is used for other purposes. The second barrier is lack of any proper study of what would constitute an optimum standard of living. I suppose that such a standard would vary for each individual and would be determined by the same criteria as health standards are today—by appropriate use of material comforts (comparable to intake of food and medicines) suited to a person's occupation and his situation among friends and family (comparable to a person's biological makeup) within a supportive social environment (comparable to climatic and other conditions in which we live). This proper study will some day yield the economic consumption requirements for the world's people, changing as new members of that population replace those who die, which then will be translated into actual orders for goods and services. All this is hardly more than economic planning and in no way precludes competition to produce efficiently, or rewards for the winners, or any other usual virtues of free enterprise. Political structures need not be altered in any respect from those indicated in my model. But determination of standards of living for each individual would alter the sense of economic justice presently in vogue, that of equal or more equal opportunities for consumption.

Similarly I ignore the whole matter of courts, judicial systems, and the appropriateness of penalties as if these were no essential part of any polity or of justice securable therein. I take it that alternative administrations of justice are as parochial as alternative procedures of any other sort; and that reconciliation of the various systems of laws in this world is no part of a general theory. Only the broadest notions of justice are appropriate in general theory just as are only the broadest notions of other aspects of a polity. But my view of justice radically departs from accepted formulas. If justice be pictured as abstract, blind to individual differences among persons, a balancing of material or other circumstances in a set of scales held by an impartial female figure, then it has no private or personal significance for us whose very humanity consists in our differences, our partiality, and our needs for reassurance, not in cool indifference. Therefore I proposed something entirely original, avoiding at all costs that barren notion of equality which has made justice an accountant's balance sheet. Yet, there is every difficulty with my notion of justice. A criminal would have to be reassured that he rightly murdered my mother, and I must be reassured that I rightly hate my mother's murderer; the warmonger is reassured and the pacifist also. How can this fail to make political consensus all the more difficult if not impossible? I accept that difficulty; justice cannot always be done. Yet I want to leave open the insight that each of us in our own ways is always right; we all know that. How must this appear before some ultimate judgment seat? I can only appeal to an image of God who must understand us every one, must be able to comfort us, "lift us up," set us on our feet, without being able to alter what we have done to ourselves. He must find us all mistaken but recognize our errors for what they are in fact, mere tempers and tempests of very limited creatures for whom He has to speak in the same way that each of us in justice should try to speak for one another, reassuring one another. Until we begin to conceive of justice in this intimate way, there can be no justice suited to a population of deficient persons.

Finally, many will say, "But we do not see how you have assured individuals or even whole populations of any real freedom from government tyranny or from one another's cruelty, cupidity, hatreds—you even think that human rights are useless unless voluntarily granted by each of us to each other—and you offer no guarantees of anyone's moral behavior. Are you a totalitarian? Where is your liberalism?" And I answer that I merely defend political morality (not every other sort, though I would do that also if it were part of the book's design), guarantee nothing, especially not personal happiness. Political morality is possible and necessary, though its necessity in no way assures it. That is the character of the human situation. I suppose that if God could guarantee morality and happiness, He would do so. I reject quite a number of historically recent ideas, especially individual autonomy, inherent political rights including freedom from others' interference, and people's capacity collectively to rule themselves. But I have no ax to grind, no preference for this result; I am merely brought to this sad conclusion because that is how matters appear to be, despite my desires for a perfect world. But I do not therefore conclude that morality is haphazard or accidental or that happiness is unobtainable. Morality is a matter of insight, of happy relationships, of the logic in human affairs, and its political potentiality always needs sober defense.